YALE CLASSICAL MONOGRAPHS, 3

DRAKON
AND
EARLY
ATHENIAN
HOMICIDE LAW

MICHAEL GAGARIN

NEW HAVEN AND LONDON   YALE UNIVERSITY PRESS

Designed by James J. Johnson
and set in IBM Press Roman type.
Printed in the Unites States of America by
The Alpine Press, Stoughton, Mass.

Library of Congress Cataloging in Publication Data

Gagarin, Michael.
    Drakon and early Athenian homicide law.

    (Yale classical monographs; 3)
    Includes bibliographical references and indexes.
      1. Homicide (Greek law)   2. Draco.   I. Title.
II. Series.

Law	345.495'0252	81-2370
ISBN 0-300-02627-7	344.950525	AACR2

10 9 8 7 6 5 4 3 2 1

FOR DONNA

CONTENTS

PREFACE

The germ of this monograph was an idea I had about the opening sentence of Drakon's law when I first encountered it as a graduate student. While I was visiting at Berkeley during 1976–77, I set out to present my idea in a short paper, but I quickly found that the answer to one question about the law raised an almost unending series of further questions. The present work certainly has not answered all of these, but I hope it may provide a basis for as well as an incentive to further study of the law and of Greek law in general.

For criticism and advice during the several years I worked on this project I am especially grateful to Ronald Stroud and Martin Ostwald. Both read more than one version of the work, and despite their disagreement with some of my views encouraged me at every stage. Alan Boegehold and Thomas Rosenmeyer also read parts of the work and made a number of helpful comments. I should also like to thank the faculty and students of the Berkeley Classics Department, and in particular Ron Stroud and Tom Rosenmeyer, for making my year there such a pleasant and productive one.

I am also grateful to the *Yale Classical Studies* Monographs Committee, and especially to Thomas Cole for his advice and encouragement. Victor Bers read the work for the committee and made many useful suggestions. At Yale University Press Sharon Slodki has been very helpful on editorial matters.

Finally, I thank the University of California Press for permission to use copyrighted material.

ABBREVIATIONS

Aly = W. Aly. *Formprobleme der frühen griechischen Prosa.*
   Philologus, Supplement 21.3 (1929).
ATL = B. D. Meritt, H. T. Wade-Gery, M. F. McGregor.
   The Athenian Tribute Lists. 4 vols. Cambridge, Mass.
   1939–53.
Bloch = A. Bloch. "Literarische und inschriftliche
   Gesetzesprosa im Griechischen." *MH* 32 (1975):135–
   54.
Bonner and Smith = R. J. Bonner and G. Smith. *The
   Administration of Justice from Homer to Aristotle.*
   2 vols. Chicago, 1930–38.
Busolt-Swoboda = G. Busolt and H. Swoboda. *Griechische
   Staatskunde,* vol. 2. Munich, 1926.
Cantarella = E. Cantarella. *Studi sull'omicidio in diritto
   greco e romano.* Milan, 1976.
Denniston, *GP* = J. D. Denniston. *The Greek Particles.* 2d
   ed. Oxford, 1954.
Denniston, *GPS* = J. D. Denniston. *Greek Prose Style.*
   Oxford, 1952.
Diamond = A. Diamond. *Primitive Law Past and Present.*
   London, 1971.
FGH = F. Jacoby. *Die Fragmente der griechischen His-
   toriker,* vols. 1–3. Berlin and Leiden, 1923–58.
Gagarin, *Drama* = M. Gagarin. *Aeschylean Drama.* Berkeley,
   1976.
Gagarin, "Self-defense" = M. Gagarin. "Self-defense in
   Athenian Homicide Law." *GRBS* 19 (1978): 111–20.

GD = C. D. Buck. *The Greek Dialects.* Chicago, 1955.

GHI = *A Selection of Greek Historical Inscriptions.* 2 vols.
  Vol. 1, ed. Russell Meiggs and David Lewis; vol. 2,
  ed. M. N. Tod. Oxford, 1948–69.

Glotz = G. Glotz. *La solidarité de la famille dans le droit
  criminel en Grèce.* Paris, 1904.

Hansen = M. H. Hansen. *Apagoge, Endeixis, and Ephegesis
  against Kakourgoi, Atimoi, and Pheugontes.* Odense,
  Denmark, 1976.

Harrison = A. R. W. Harrison. *The Law of Athens.* 2 vols.
  Oxford, 1968–71.

Hignett = C. Hignett. *A History of the Athenian Constitu-
  tion.* Oxford, 1952.

IC = *Inscriptiones Creticae,* vol. 4, ed. M. Guarducci.
  Rome, 1950.

IGS = *Inscriptiones Graecae Siciliae et Infimae Italiae ad
  Ius Pertinentes,* ed. V. A. Ruiz and A. Olivieri. Milan,
  1925.

IJG = *Recueil des inscriptions juridiques grecques.* 2 vols.
  Ed. R. Dareste, B. Hassoullier, and T. Reinach. Paris,
  1891–1904.

Loomis = W. T. Loomis. "The Nature of Premeditation in
  Athenian Homicide Law." *JHS* 92 (1972): 86–95.

LS = *Lois sacrées des cités grecques.* Ed. F. Sokolowski.
  Paris, 1969.

MacDowell = D. M. MacDowell. *Athenian Homicide Law
  in the Age of the Orators.* Manchester, 1963.

Maschke = R. Maschke. *Die Willenslehre im griechischen
  Recht.* Berlin, 1926.

Meiggs-Lewis. See *GHI.*

Moulinier = L. Moulinier. *Le pur et l'impur dans la pensée
  des Grecs.* Paris, 1952.

Ostwald = M. Ostwald. "The Athenian Legislation against
  Tyranny and Subversion." *TAPA* 86 (1955): 103–28.

RIG = C. Michel. *Recueil d'inscriptions grecques.* Brussels,
  1900.

Ruschenbusch, *"phonos"* = E. Ruschenbusch. "ΦΟΝΟΣ: zum Recht Drakons und seiner Bedeutung für das Werden des athenischen Staates." *Historia* 9 (1960): 129–54.

Ruschenbusch, *SN* = E. Ruschenbusch. ΣΟΛΩΝΟΣ NOMOI. *Historia,* Einzelschriften 9. Wiesbaden, 1966.

Sealey = R. Sealey. *A History of the Greek City States 700–333 B.C.* Berkeley, 1976.

SEG = *Supplementum Epigraphicum Graecum.*

SN. See Ruschenbusch, *SN.*

Steinwenter = A. Steinwenter. *Die Streitbeendigung durch Urteil, Schiedsspruch, und Vergleich nach griechischem Rechte.* Munich, 1925.

Stroud = R. S. Stroud. *Drakon's Law on Homicide.* Berkeley, 1968.

Willetts = R. F. Willetts. *The Law Code of Gortyn.* Berlin, 1967.

Wolff = H. J. Wolff. "The Origin of Judicial Litigation among the Greeks." *Traditio* 4 (1946): 31–87.

Orators:

Ais. = Aischines   Isok. = Isokrates
And. = Andokides   Lyk. = Lykourgos
Ant. = Antiphon   Lys. = Lysias
Dem. = Demosthenes

For purposes of reference I do not distinguish between speeches truly or falsely ascribed to a particular author.

THE TEXT OF DRAKON'S LAW

IG I².115 (I³.104), lines 1–41*

Διόγν[ε]τος Φρεάρριος ἐγραμμάτε[υε]

Διοκλῆς ἔρχε

ἔδοχσεν τῆι βουλῆι καὶ τῶι δέμοι· Ἀκα[μ]αντὶς ἐπ[ρ]υτάνευε,[Δ]ιό[γ]-
νετος ἐγραμμάτευε,Εὐθύδικος [ἐ]πεστάτε,..Ε...ΑΝΕΣ εἶπε· τὸ[ν]
5 Δράκοντος νόμον τὸμ περὶ τõ φό[ν]ο ἀναγρα[φ]σά[ν]τον οἱ ἀναγραφε͂-
ς τὸν νόμον παραλαβόντες παρὰ τõ β[α]σ[ι]λέ[ος με]τ[ὰ τõ γραμμ]ατέο-
ς τε͂ς βουλε͂ς ἐ' στέλει λιθίνει καὶ κα[τ]α[θ]έντ[ον πρόσ]θε[ν] τε͂ς στο-
ᾶς τε͂ς βασιλείας· οἱ δὲ πολεταὶ ἀπομι[σθο]σ[άντον κατὰ τὸν ν]όμο-
ν, οἱ δὲ ἑλλενοταμίαι δόντον τὸ ἀρ[γ]ύ[ρ]ι[ον].
10 Πρõτος ''Αχσον
κ_αὶ ἐὰμ μὲ 'κ [π]ρονοί[α]ς̲ [κ]τ̲[ένει τίς τινα, φεύγ]ε[ν·δ]ι-
κάζεν δὲ τὸς βασιλέας αἴτιο[ν] φόν[ο] Ε............¹⁷........Ε [β]ολ-
εύσαντα·τὸς δὲ ἐφέτας διαγν[õ]ν[α]ι̣. [αἰδέσασθαι δ' ἐὰμ μὲν πατέ]ρ ε͂-
ι ἒ ἀδελφὸ[ς] ἒ hυε͂ς, hάπαντ[α]ς, ἒ τὸν κο[λύοντα κρατε͂ν· ἐὰν δὲ μὲ] hοῦ-
15 τοι ὀσι̣, μέχρ' ἀνεφ[σι]ότετος καὶ̣ [ἀνεφσιõ, ἐὰν hάπαντες αἰδέσ]ασ-
θαι ἐθέλοσι, τὸν κο[λύ]οντ̲α [κ]ρα[τε͂ν· ἐὰν δὲ τούτον·μεδὲ hε͂ς ἔι, κτ]έ-
νει δὲ ἄκο[ν], γνõσι δὲ hοι̣ [πε]ντ[έκοντα καὶ hε͂ς hοι ἐφέται ἄκοντ]α
κτε͂ναι, ἐσέσ̲θ[ο]ν δὲ h̲[οι φ]ρ[άτορες ἐὰν ἐθέλοσι δέκα· τούτος δ]ὲ h̲ο̲-
ι πεντέκο[ν]τ̲[α καὶ] hε͂ς ἀρ[ι]στ̲[ίνδεν haιρέσθον. καὶ hοι.δὲ πρ]ότε[ρ]-
20 ον κτέ[ν]α̣[ντ]ε[ς ἐν] τõ[ιδε τõι θεσμõι ἐνεχέσθον. προειπε͂ν δ]ὲ τõι κ-
τέ̲ν̲α̲ν̲[τι ἐν ἀ]γορ[ᾶι μέχρ' ἀνεφσιότετος καὶ ἀνεφσιõ· συνδιόκ]εν
δὲ [κ]ἀνεφσ[ιὸς καὶ ἀνεφσιõν παῖδας καὶ γαμβρὸς καὶ πενθερὸ]ς κ-
αὶ φρ[ά]τ̲[ο]ρ̲[ας...............³⁶............. αἴτιος [ἔι] φό[νο.....................²⁶........... τὸς πεντέκοντ]α καὶ
25 hένα............................⁴²............. φόνο
hέλοσ[ι....................³⁵.............ἐὰν δ]έ [τ]ις τ-
ὸ[ν ἀν]δ̲ρ[οφόνον κτένει ἒ αἴτιος ἔι φόνο, ἀπεχόμενον ἀγορᾶ]ς ἐφο-
ρί[α]ς κ̲[α]ὶ̣ [ἄθλον καὶ hιερõν Ἀμφικτυονικõν, hόσπερ τὸν Ἀθεν]αῖον κ-
[τένα]ν̲[τα, ἐν τοῖς αὐτοῖς ἐνέχεσθαι· διαγιγνόσκεν δὲ τὸς] ἐ[φ]έτα[ς]
30 ...Ε.............................³⁹.............. Τ̲ΕΙΕΜΕΔ

---

*Reprinted with permission from R. S. Stroud, *Drakon's Law on Homicide* (Berkeley and Los Angeles, 1968), p. 5.

xiv

```
  .........................⁴⁵.................ΟΝΑΤ.
  ........................·⁴⁵·.................ΑΝΑ..
Ν...........................³⁹............ ἄρχον]τα χερ-
ὸν ἀ[δίκον............................³⁰.......... χερ]ὸν ἀδίκον κ-
τέ[νει.......]Σ̣[...................¹⁹....διαγιγνόσκ]εν δὲ τὸς ἐ-
[φέτ]as.........................··³⁶..............ΕΙΣΕ ἐλεύθ-
ε[ρ]ος ἐι. κα̣[ὶ ἐὰν φέροντα ἒ ἄγοντα βίαι ἀδίκος εὐθὺs] ἀμυνόμενο-
s κτέ[ν]ει, ν[εποινὲ τεθνάναι. . . .¹⁹.............ΣΕΧΟΝΤΟΒ.
ΙΑΝ..Α̣...........................³⁵..............τ]ὲν ἀπόστα-
σιν ΤΟ̣.............·-.............³⁷......ΕΣ δεκατε̣-
s]ΤΟ..Ι........................³⁷.................Ε ΔΕΚΑ..
```

Addenda: line 12, read: ἒ[ναι τὸν ἐργασάμενον] ἒ vel sim.
lines 30–31, read: [ἐχσ]ἒ[ναι δὲ τὸς ἀνδροφόνος
ἀποκτένεν ἒ ἀπάγεν, ἐὰν ἐν] τἕι ἐμεδ[απἕι...
(Stroud) vel sim.

TRANSLATION

Diognetos of the deme Phrearrioi was secretary
Diokles was archon
Resolved by the boule and the demos, Akamantis held
the prytany, Diognetos was secretary, Euthydikos
was chairman, . . . made the motion: Let the scribes
5   inscribe Drakon's law on homicide on a marble
stele, taking it from the basileus with the help of the
secretary of the boule, and let them set it in front
of the Stoa Basileios. Let the poletai contract for the
work according to law, and let the hellenotamiai
pay the money.

10   FIRST AXON
Even if a man not intentionally kills another, he
is exiled. The basileis are to adjudge responsible for
homicide either the actual killer or the planner; and
the Ephetai are to judge the case. If there is a father
or brother or sons, pardon is to be agreed to by all,
or the one who opposes is to prevail; but if none of
15   these survives, by those up to the degree of first
cousin once removed and first cousin, if all are willing
to agree to a pardon; the one who opposes is to prevail; but if not one of these survives, and if he killed
unintentionally and the fifty-one, the Ephetai, decide
he killed unintentionally, let ten phratry members
admit him to the country and let the fifty-one choose
20   these by rank. And let also those who killed previously
be bound by this law. A proclamation is to be made

against the killer in the agora by the victim's relatives
as far as the degree of cousin's son and cousin. The
prosecution is to be shared by the cousins and cousins'
sons and by sons-in-law, fathers-in-law, and phratry
members . . . is responsible for homicide . . . the fifty-
25 one . . . is convicted of homicide . . . If anyone kills
the killer or is responsible for his death, as long as he
stays away from the frontier markets, games, and
Amphiktyonic sacrifices, he shall be liable to the same
treatment as the one who kills an Athenian; and the
30 Ephetai are to judge the case. It is allowed to kill or
arrest killers, if they are caught in the territory . . .
starting a fight . . . kills . . . and the Ephetai are to
35 judge the case . . . is a free man, and if he defending
himself straightway kills someone forcibly and unjustly plundering or seizing him, the victim shall die
without the killer paying a penalty.

DRAKON AND
EARLY ATHENIAN HOMICIDE LAW

CHAPTER ONE

INTRODUCTION

In 409/8 B.C., during a period of general investigation into and revision of the laws of their city, the Athenians passed a decree authorizing the publication on a stele of "Drakon's law on homicide," originally written by the lawgiver Drakon[1] in about 621/0.[2] Part of the stele, which was erected at the Stoa Basileios, still survives (*IG* I².115 [I³.104]), and though badly damaged preserves most of the decree and portions of the beginning of the law. It was published several times in the nineteenth century, most notably by M. Köhler,[3] and since its discovery the substance and significance of the law have been widely discussed and at times hotly disputed by students of Greek legal and constitutional history.

Surprisingly, the stone itself was ignored for nearly a

---

1. Beloch's theory that Drakon was not a man but a sacred serpent has recently been revived by Sealey, p. 104. In reply to Sealey's arguments one should say first that the supposition of a religious source and a long period of development behind the homicide law, even if true, is not incompatible with the existence of a single human lawgiver; and second that "Athens' exceptional position of having two early lawgivers, where the other states had only one" is in fact an argument for Drakon's historical existence, since the tradition would have been more likely to reduce two early figures to one than vice versa. If the history of early Athens appears exceptional, must we rewrite it? See also Stroud, pp. 65–66.

2. For the date see Stroud, pp. 66–70.

3. *Hermes* 2 (1867): 27–36.

century until Ronald Stroud undertook to clean and re-
examine it. The text that he published in 1968[4] is a significant improvement over Köhler's text and establishes a
more secure basis for discussion of the law. Moreover,
Stroud's epigraphical and historical commentaries on the
text provide a fund of valuable information, and many
of his conclusions, especially on epigraphical matters, seem
indisputable. Stroud's study is the starting point for all
future work on Drakon's law, and I shall refer to it often
in the following pages.

In spite of Stroud's achievement, problems concerning
the interpretation and significance of the law still remain.
In particular, the most disputed feature of Drakon's law,
that it apparently begins with a law on unintentional homicide without mentioning intentional homicide, has still
not been satisfactorily explained. My primary aim in this
study is to provide a detailed discussion of the surviving
or restorable provisions of the law in the light of both earlier and later Athenian homicide law, to the extent that
we can reconstruct it. I shall also examine at length the
question of the original position and content of the law on
intentional homicide and shall suggest a new solution.
Finally, I shall consider the law as a whole and shall try to
assess Drakon's achievement as a lawgiver.

Although I shall generally avoid the use of modern
terms such as *murder* and *manslaughter,* it may prove helpful to delineate briefly the modern categories of homicide
and to set beside them the fourth-century Athenian categories. Current American laws on homicide treat it in six
general categories: [5]

---

4. *Drakon's Law on Homicide* (Berkeley, 1968). Stroud discovered 218 new letters on the stone.

5. These categories correspond to Loomis's five categories
(pp. 88–89), except that I divide murder into two degrees, as is done

a. first-degree murder (premeditated homicide);
b. second-degree murder (homicide with intent to kill or harm but without premeditation);
c. voluntary manslaughter (unpremeditated but intentional homicide with severe provocation);
d. involuntary manslaughter (unintentional homicide resulting from negligence or from an unlawful act);
e. justified homicide (e.g., in self-defense);
f. accidental homicide.

The first four categories are punished with decreasing severity; in the last two the killer is considered innocent of any crime.

In order to delineate the Athenian categories of homicide it is easiest to use the categorization by courts, which the Athenians themselves used (Dem. 23.65–75, Arist. *Ath. Pol.* 57.3). There were three major categories: [6]

1. intentional homicide, [7] which was tried at the Areopagos;
2. unintentional homicide, which was tried at the Palladion;
3. lawful homicide, [8] which was tried at the Delphinion.

---

in most American states. For this outline I have relied on W. R. LaFave and A. W. Scott, *Handbook on Criminal Law* (St. Paul, Minn., 1972), pp. 528–602.

6. Two other special homicide courts are not relevant here: the Prytaneion, where unknown or nonhuman killers were tried, and the courts at Phreatto, where killers already in exile for unintentional homicide were tried.

7. For the distinction between intentional and unintentional homicide see below, pp. 31–37.

8. I use the term *lawful homicide* to designate the category of homicides that were not punished. We do not know the precise designation of this category in Athenian law; see Gagarin, "Self-defense," p. 112, n. 7.

The penalties for intentional homicide were death or exile and confiscation of property, and for unintentional homicide exile, perhaps for a limited period.[9] Lawful homicide carried no penalty.

A rough correspondence between these two systems can be set forth as follows: (1) intentional homicide would include (a), (b), and those cases of (c) and (e) in which the provocation would not be such as to justify a plea of lawful homicide or of self-defense;[10] (2) unintentional homicide would include (d) and (f), unless one could show that the accidental death was the victim's fault (as the accused in Antiphon's *Second Tetralogy* tries to do); (3) lawful homicide would include many cases of (c), in which the type of provocation (e.g., adultery) justifies the killing, and some cases of (f), such as killing an opponent in an athletic contest. With regard to severity, the two systems are about equal: the Athenians punished cases of accidental homicide, which we do not (though the arguments in Antiphon's *Second Tetralogy* suggest that unintentional homicide normally was thought to involve some negligence, however slight); on the other hand, we punish certain cases of provoked homicide, such as the killing of an adulterer, which the Athenians did not, and until recently we commonly executed murderers, whereas exile was the more common penalty for intentional homicide in Athens (see below, pp. 112–15.

---

9. See MacDowell, pp. 122–23.

10. Killing in self-defense was probably not considered a case of lawful homicide but was grounds for acquittal on a charge of intentional homicide; see Gagarin, "Self-defense."

CHAPTER TWO

HOMICIDE LAW BEFORE AND AFTER DRAKON

Before examining Drakon's law, it will be helpful first to set forth the evidence, scarce though it may be, on two subjects, the treatment of homicide before Drakon's time and the transmission of his law to the fifth and fourth centuries.

We have no inscriptional or other direct evidence for the treatment of homicide in Athens before the passage of Drakon's law, and we must thus rely on inferences from the indirect evidence of epic poetry, from Drakon's law itself, and from our scanty historical knowledge of pre-Drakontian Athens. There are, of course, difficulties in using the epic material, which reflects the culture of a wide area and may not correspond precisely to any actual historical culture, but several considerations prompt the attempt. First of all, the body of Homeric and other early epic literature depicts a generally consistent social organization that probably reflects conditions in the ninth century[1] and thus is likely to have provided the general background for Athenian customs of the seventh century. More specifically, although the consequences of a homicide in the poems are not the same in every case, they are fully consistent with one another and may easily be understood as forming a single system. Furthermore, we shall see that certain elements in Drakon's law point

---

1. See M. I. Finley, *The World of Odysseus,* 2d ed. (New York, 1978), esp. pp. 142–58; cf. E. A. Havelock, *The Greek Concept of Justice* (Cambridge, Mass., 1978), pp. 55–87.

implicitly to the preexistence of the very system we can reconstruct on the basis of the epic evidence. In view of these considerations, it is worthwhile to determine as fully as possible the methods of dealing with homicide that are portrayed in the epics, even if we cannot demonstrate with certainty that such methods existed in pre-Drakontian Athens.

The following is a list of all homicides committed or contemplated in the epic poems.[2] Killing in battle is excluded from these examples, even though a desire for vengeance was also felt by those whose relatives died on the battlefield.[3] First is a list of actual homicides:

1. *Il.* 2.661–70: Tlepolemos killed his father's maternal uncle and, threatened by others, went into exile in Rhodes; Zeus showered wealth on him.
2. *Il.* 13.694–97 (cf. 15.333–36): Medon killed the brother of his stepmother and is living in exile.
3. *Il.* 15.431–39: Lykophron killed a man and came to live with Ajax, where he was greatly honored.
4. *Il.* 16.572–75: Epigeus killed his cousin and joined Achilles' forces.
5. *Il.* 18.497–508: On Achilles' shield a trial is being held concerning compensation for a man who was killed.
6. *Il.* 23.85–90: Patroklos, when a boy, killed another boy in anger (χολωθείς) over a dice game but not wishing to (οὐκ ἐθέλων); he goes into exile and joins Achilles.
7. *Il.* 24.480–83: In a simile the wonder (θάμβος) felt

2. I include in this discussion the poems in the epic cycle, [Hesiod's] *Shield of Heracles,* and the Hesiodic fragments.
3. See *Il.* 14.482–85.

by Achilles beholding the suppliant Priam is compared to the wonder of onlookers beholding an exiled killer who seeks protection at the court of a rich man.

8. *Od.* 1.35–43, etc.:[4] Aigisthos killed Agamemnon and was later killed by Orestes.

9. *Od.* 11.422–30: Klytaimestra killed Kassandra and assisted with the killing of Agamemnon;[5] she was later killed[6] and buried by Orestes.

10. *Od.* 3.309–10, etc.: Orestes killed Aigisthos and Klytaimestra and is much praised for it.

11. *Od.* 4.536–37: The followers of Agamemnon and Aigisthos all killed each other.

12. *Od.* 11.273–80: Oidipous killed his own father (unknowingly); the deed was brought to light; he continued to rule Thebes but suffered many woes brought on by his mother's Furies (i.e., the result of incest, not of parricide).

13. *Od.* 13.259–75: According to one of Odysseus's false tales, he was deprived of his share of some

---

4. For the story of Agamemnon's death and Orestes' revenge in the *Odyssey* see 1. 29–30, 35–43, 298–300; 3.193–98, 234–35, 248–52, 255–75, 303–10; 4.91–92, 519–37, 546–47; 11.387–89, 409–34; 24.20–22, 96–97, 199–202.

5. Klytaimestra's precise role in the death of Agamemnon is not clear, but it appears that Aigisthos was the actual killer (1.35–36, 4.534–35, etc.) and that she only assisted him (3.235, 11.410, 11.429–30), though in 24.200 she is spoken of as having killed him (κουρίδιον κτείνασα πόσιν).

6. The killing of Klytaimestra is not explicitly mentioned, though it is clearly alluded to in 3.310 (cf. Stanford's note *ad loc.*). It is almost certain, moreover, that she was killed as punishment for her part in the killing of Agamemnon and not for killing Kassandra, whose death would not be avenged in Mycenae.

booty (because of insubordination); he killed a man
in ambush at night; and though not seen by anyone,
he immediately left the country.

14. *Od.* 14.380–81: An unnamed Aitolian, a fugitive
killer, was hospitably entertained by Eumaios.

15. *Od.* 15.271–82 (cf. 15.224): Theoklymenos killed
a fellow tribesman in Argos and is a fugitive in Pylos;
he is welcomed on board by Telemachos.

16. *Od.* 21.24–30: Herakles killed his guest Iphitos for
his horses; there was no punishment.

17. *Od.* 22.1–33: Odysseus kills Antinoos. The suitors
think he did so by mistake (οὐκ ἐθέλοντα) and intend
to kill him in return.

18. *Od.* 22: Odysseus and Telemachos kill the suitors,
after which (24.430–37) their relatives demand vengeance and hope to kill Odysseus and Telemachos
before they can get away from the country. Athena
stops them, but not before Odysseus has killed
Antinoos's father, Eupeithes (24.522–25).

19. *Od.* 22.465–72: Telemachos kills twelve maid-
servants and Melanthios; no punishment follows.

20. Proclus, *Chrest.* 2: In the *Aithiopis* Achilles killed
Thersites (who reviled him); there was a dispute
among the Achaians; Achilles went to Lesbos, sacri-
ficed, and was purified by Odysseus.

21. Photios, *Lex.* (= Suda) s.v. Τευμησία: In the
Epigonoi Kephalos, an Athenian, killed his own wife
unintentionally (ἄκων) and was purified by the
Cadmians.

22. [Hesiod] *Shield* 9–19, 80–85; Amphitryon killed
his father-in-law in a dispute over cattle; he went
into exile with his wife and was much honored in
Thebes.

23. Hesiod fr. 257: Hyettos killed an adulterer, went

into exile, and was honored with a portion of his host's estate, "as is proper" (ὡς ἐπιεικές).

In addition to these, one homicide is attempted without success and four are contemplated or imagined but not carried out:

24. *Od.* 4.669–74, 16.374–405, etc.: The suitors attempt to kill Telemachos. The people of Ithaka would be angry if they knew about this and would expel the suitors (16.380–82).
25. *Il.* 6.167–90: Proitos shrinks from killing Bellerophontes and sends him to his father-in-law, who tries unsuccessfully to have him killed.
26. *Il.* 9.458–61: Phoinix wanted to kill his father but desisted because of the bad reputation which comes to patricides.
27. *Il.* 24.583–86: Achilles takes precautions so that he will not disobey Zeus and kill Priam in anger.
28. *Od.* 14.402–06: Eumaios, if he were to kill his guest (the disguised Odysseus), would suffer ill fame and would pray to Zeus.

Finally, several general remarks about the treatment of homicide are important:

29. *Il.* 9.632–36, Ajax to Achilles: A man whose brother or child is killed accepts blood money (ποινή) and his anger is calmed, and the killer remains in the country.
30. *Od.* 3.196–97: It is a good thing for a man who is killed to leave a son behind to avenge his death (as Orestes avenges Agamemnon's death).
31. *Od.* 23.118–22, Odysseus to Telemachos: When a

man kills another man who has even a few relatives
to take vengeance, he flees the country.

From this list is is clear that the most common result
of a homicide in the epics is that the killer flees and goes
into exile.[7] It is apparent also from the examples of
Theoklymenos (no. 15) and others that this flight is the
direct consequence of the necessity to escape death at
the hands of the victim's relatives seeking revenge, and
although it is likely that this desire for revenge was stronger
in some cases than in others,[8] the threat of vengeance
probably lay ultimately behind every case of exile for homicide. Only in cases in which there is no threat of vengeance from the victim's relatives, as when Herakles kills
his guest Iphitos (no. 16), does the killer not go into exile
or otherwise compensate the relatives.[9] It is particularly
notable that Oidipous (no. 12) continues to rule Thebes
after killing his father; being his victim's closest relative,
he would have been under no threat of vengeance.
    The example of Theoklymenos, who is in Pylos fleeing
from Argives, also indicates that the relatives could pursue
a killer beyond the borders of their home territory. Thus, a
killer was a fugitive until he was accepted by someone in
another country, as Theoklymenos is accepted by Telem-

---

7. See nos. 1, 2, 3, 4, 6, 7, 13, 14, 15, 22, 23, 24, 31.
8. Cf., e.g., nos. 6 and 18.
9. See nos. 10, 19, 20, 28. In nos. 8 and 9 the killers (foolishly)
do not anticipate Orestes' revenge and thus do not flee; in no. 18
only divine intervention permits the killing to remain unavenged. In
Od. 1.376–80 (= 2.141–45) Telemachos, angered at the suitors'
behavior, vows to pray to Zeus and send παλίντιτα ἔργα, "for then
you would perish in this house unavenged" (νήποινοί κεν ἔπειτα
δόμων ἔντοσθεν ὄλοισθε). Telemachos may be referring to the possibility of homicide without compensation (as in fact actually happens),
but he is more likely thinking of a divine rather than human action.

achos. The suppliant killer was a common figure (no. 7), and after being accepted in his new land the killer was often not only protected but even honored.[10] The killer had wronged the victim's family and they were entitled to their vengeance, but once he had been accepted into a new society, he apparently bore no moral stigma on account of his deed, though of course his lack of property in his new land would tend to limit the power and status he could attain.[11]

There is no evidence that the intentionality of the homicide was a factor in the treatment of the killer. In many cases there is no indication of intent; where it is indicated, usually only by implication, the killing is almost always intentional.[12] The best evidence for the treatment of unintentional homicide is the episode of Odysseus's killing of Antinoos (no. 17), which the other suitors at first assume to have been unintentional (οὐκ ἐθέλοντα, 22.31);[13] even so, they declare, he must die for it. This example indicates that there was no fundamental difference in the treatment of intentional and unintentional homicide in the epics (see below, n. 24).[14]

---

10. See nos. 1, 3, 6, 15, 22, 23.

11. In some cases (no. 23) the exiled killer may be granted an estate of his own (cf. no. 1); more often he becomes someone's steward or companion. This attitude toward killers may have continued into Solon's time if Plutarch's report is true (*Sol.* 24.4) that Solon granted Athenian citizenship to two categories of immigrants, one of which was those in permanent exile from their own country (τοῖς φεύγουσιν ἀειφυγίᾳ τὴν ἑαυτῶν), since this category presumably included some who were in exile for homicide.

12. See nos. 6, 8, 9, 10, 11, 13, 16, 18, 20, 22, 23.

13. The same expression occurs in Patroklos's case (no. 6), but there the presence of the further qualification χολωθείς differentiates his case from the killing of Antinoos, which at first is considered a pure accident.

14. Cf. Maschke, p. 6, and A. W. H. Adkins, *Merit and Responsi-*

Daube disputes this conclusion[15] and observes that
"the sources offer not one example of an unintentional
killer being killed" (p. 174). We should bear in mind, of
course, that the Greek sources also offer very few examples
of an intentional killer's being killed. Furthermore, Daube's
view that the killing of Antinoos is considered intentional
by the other suitors cannot stand: the tale of the drunken
centaur (21.295–304), more than a hundred lines earlier,
stresses the danger of drink but does not imply that the
same degree of intentionality underlies a drunken rape and
a drunken accident; Odysseus's statement that he will hit
an unusual target is clearly not understood by the suitors
to mean he will kill Antinoos; the suitors look for arms to
protect themselves from someone shooting at random,
since it is possible that another accident will occur; and
finally, Patroklos's case is clearly different (see above,
n. 13).

The fact that in the epics the basic treatment of intentional and unintentional homicide is the same is consistent
with the general lack of concern with intent in the punishment of wrongdoing which the poems reveal.[16] This is not

---

bility (Oxford, 1960), p. 53. I do not mean to imply that the Greeks
did not know the difference between intentional and unintentional
action, only that their response to intentional and unintentional
homicide was essentially the same.

15. David Daube, *Roman Law: Linguistic, Social, and Philosoph-
ical Aspects* (Edinburgh, 1969), pp. 163–75.

16. See Gagarin, *Drama*, pp. 7–11. A similar lack of concern with
intent seems to characterize certain tribal societies, though some
anthropologists are now aware that the issue is too complex to be
discussed simply in terms of either strict liability or full (moral)
responsibility. See, e.g., Max Gluckman, *The Ideas in Barotse Juris-
prudence* (New Haven, 1965), pp. 204–41, and S. F. Moore, *Law
as Process* (London, 1978), pp. 82–134; Moore suggests there is a
connection between strict liability and self-help (pp. 98–99).

to say that there were no differences; for instance, the victim's relatives may have been more likely to allow the unintentional killer to go into exile without attempting to kill him, and they may also have been more willing to agree to a monetary settlement. But the basic system of punishment or compensation applied to all cases of homicide, regardless of intent.

Monetary compensation for homicide, or blood money (ποινή), though common in other early societies, is rare in the Greek epics. Ajax admonishes Achilles (no. 29) to relent since others whose relatives are killed relent and accept blood money "and the killer remains in the country," but the only actual example of monetary compensation for homicide is found in the trial scene on Achilles' shield (no. 5).[17]

Many details of this trial have been disputed,[18] but I shall here be concerned only with the nature of the dispute. The issue is described as follows (Il. 18.498–500):

> δύο δ᾽ ἄνδρες ἐνείκεον εἵνεκα ποινῆς
> ἀνδρὸς ἀποφθιμένου. ὁ μὲν εὔχετο πάντ᾽ ἀποδοῦναι
> δήμῳ πιφαύσκων, ὁ δ᾽ ἀναίνετο μηδὲν ἑλέσθαι.

It is clear from the first lines that the killer is known and that the trial concerns not the homicide itself but the monetary compensation due the victim's relatives (εἵνεκα

---

17. There may be a reference to monetary compensation at the end of the Odyssey, where Athena bids the suitors' relatives to stop fighting with Odysseus "so that you may quickly settle the matter without bloodshed" (ὥς κεν ἀναιμωτί γε διακρινθῆτε τάχιστα, 24.532).

18. Among the many treatments of this famous scene see Steinwenter, pp. 34–38; Bonner and Smith, vol. 1, pp. 31–41; Wolff, pp. 36–49; Hildebrecht Hommel, Palingenesia 4 (1969):11–38.

ποινῆς). The meaning of the second sentence (499–500) is
disputed, and two different interpretations have been
proposed: (a) one man claimed to have paid all [the blood
money], demonstrating his case to the people, but the
other denied he had received anything; and (b) one man
vowed he would pay all, setting forth his case to the people,
but the other refused to accept anything.

The first half of this sentence (ὁ μὲν εὔχετο πάντ'
ἀποδοῦναι δήμῳ πιφαύσκων) supports sense (a) for three
reasons: first, εὔχομαι with the aorist infinitive elsewhere
has this past sense; a future infinitive would be expected
for sense (b).[19] Second, πάντα implies that the dispute concerns a specific sum of money already determined; for
sense (b) one would have to understand πάντα to mean
"all that the victim's relatives might desire." Third, δήμῳ
πιφαύσκων is perhaps more easily understood with sense
(a), since one can more easily "demonstrate" that one has
done something (perhaps with the aid of witnesses) than
that one will do something. The second half of the sentence
(ὁ δ' ἀναίνετο μηδὲν ἐλέσθαι), on the other hand, supports
sense (b), since ἀναίνομαι regularly means "refuse" or "reject," not "deny," and the only other times it occurs in
epic with an infinitive (Il. 18.450, 23.204, Hes. fr. 73.4) it
clearly means "refuse."[20]

Most scholars after considering these points on both

_____

19. See Il. 4.101–02 (= 119–20), Od. 17.59–60. H. H. Pflüger
(Hermes 77 [1942]: 140–48) challenged this argument, but in
all the examples he cites (p. 142) of εὔχομαι with the aorist, the
verb means "pray" (to the gods that one might do something)
and not "vow" (that one will do something).

20. See Lexikon des frügriechischen Epos, ed. Bruno Snell, vol.
5 (Göttingen, 1967), pp. 775–76. The few examples it gives of
ἀναίνομαι in the sense of "deny" (leugnen), among which is Il.
18.500, are really extensions of the sense "reject."

sides have admitted the further consideration that, judging from our slender knowledge of "Homeric" society, a dispute would be more likely to be submitted for a public settlement if it concerned simply the amount of money paid; the decision whether or not to accept compensation in the first place was probably left to the victim's family alone. Thus, scholars have for the most part preferred sense (a). Still, there remains the difficulty concerning the sense of ἀναίνομαι, and I would like to suggest a third possibility, namely that we combine the prima facie more likely meanings of the first and second halves of the sentence as follows: "One man claimed to have paid all the blood money, demonstrating his case for the people, but the other refused to accept anything."

The difficulty with this interpretation is that it seems to make the two men argue about different issues: the first about whether the money had been paid and the second about whether any payment would be acceptable. It is possible, however, to imagine a situation that might account for the fact that the killer has already paid all the blood money, as he claims, and that the other disputant, presumably a relative of the dead man, refuses to accept any compensation at all, if we suppose that a disagreement exists between the relatives of the victim. One relative has agreed to accept compensation and has done so, but another disagrees with this decision and takes the dispute to a public forum. It is impossible to say just how such a case might proceed or what the final settlement might be, but it is a plausible hypothesis that such disagreements among the relatives arose occasionally before explicit rules such as we find in Drakon's law were laid down for the acceptance of compensation.[21] We cannot be certain that

---

21. In no. 29 Ajax says that "a man whose brother or child is killed accepts blood money," which implies that at least two dif-

a dispute among the relatives lies behind the trial scene on
Achilles' shield, but this hypothesis does fit the natural
sense of the Greek text, as we have it.

If the acceptance of blood money after a homicide
might occasionally give rise to confusion, so too might the
coexistence of the two different treatments of homicide,
exile and compensation.[22] Whatever the origins of these
two systems, they are certainly not incompatible,[23] since
within the normal pattern of pursuit and exile of the killer
the victim's relatives might occasionally moderate their
desire for revenge and accept compensation instead. But
such a system might at times lead to confusion and would
make it difficult to regulate the treatment of homicide
in an orderly way. A killer would not know whether to flee
immediately or try to arrange a monetary settlement, and
would run the risk of going needlessly into exile or, on the
other hand, of being killed while trying to arrange for
compensation. When in doubt most killers presumably
would choose exile.

---

ferent relatives were traditionally allowed to arrange for the payment.

22. We should bear in mind that exile may be the most common
penalty for homicide in the poems simply because it is most likely
to occasion comment: a dead killer is no longer of interest except in
a special case such as Aigisthos, and the fact that a man has paid
blood money in the past would usually not be worth mentioning.

23. Punishment, whether exile or death, is in fact a form of
compensation; David Daube, *Studies in Biblical Law* (Cambridge,
1947), p. 128, on the *lex talionis:* "Punishment includes restitution.
. . . Punishment itself compensates the party wronged for his loss."
Glotz, pp. 125–31, maintains that the amount of monetary compensation for homicide was enormous and that many killers, especially
poor ones, would have been forced to go into exile instead of paying
compensation. But it is unlikely that the amount of compensation
would have been large enough to prevent, say, Patroklos's father from
paying it.

It is also possible that killers regularly fled into exile first, after which monetary compensation might be arranged between the relatives of the killer and the victim, and if these parties succeeded in reaching an agreement, then the killer would return. This procedure, exile first and then compensation, seems to be implied by the order of the provisions in Drakon's law, but this is no proof that it was the regular procedure before Drakon. In short, we do not know precisely how the two systems were combined in early Athens, but it is quite likely that both existed.

The epics also shed light on several other aspects of the treatment of homicide at this time. First, the fact that Orestes takes revenge on both Klytaimestra and Aigisthos (nos. 8, 9) seems to indicate that an accomplice or conspirator in a homicide case was considered equally liable. Second, the story of Hyettos (no. 23), who in his own house killed his wife's lover Molouros and then left Argos and was received by Minyeios, who gave him a share of his estate "as is proper," indicates that the killer of an adulterer had to go into exile just like other killers. It is possible that in this case the special provocation might account for the honor with which Hyettos was received in exile, but others are similarly honored in exile (see above, n. 10), and the poet does not seem to treat this case as different from the others.

Another notable feature of the treatment of homicide in the epics is that the concept of religious pollution is almost entirely lacking. Odysseus's cleaning of his house after the slaughter of the suitors (*Od.* 22.493–94) seems to be more a sanitary precaution than a religious purification. The reports of Achilles' purification after killing Thersites in the *Aithiopis* (no. 20) and of Kephalos's purification after unintentionally killing his wife in the *Epigonoi* (no. 21) are the only possible examples of religious purification, but as Moulinier (pp. 42–43) admits, these sketchy accounts may be influenced by later ideas;

otherwise there is no hint in the epics that religious pollution was one of the consequences of homicide.[24]

Finally, we should note that despite the common assumption that vendettas were a frequent result of homicide in early Greece, no homicide in the epics gives rise to a vendetta; in fact no homicide in the epics is avenged by death except the killing of Agamemnon, and the killings of Aigisthos and Klytaimestra are not avenged in turn. The system of killing in retaliation for a homicide need not necessarily lead to a vendetta,[25] and I suspect that the unending series of retaliatory killings imagined in the *Oresteia* was conceived by Aischylos himself to fit the cyclical pattern of crimes envisioned in that trilogy.

Although we cannot know with certainty whether the method of treating homicide portrayed in the epics actually was common in pre-Drakontian Athens, there are several indications in Drakon's law itself that the treatment of homicide before Drakon was similar to that found in the epics. These indications do not prove a direct link between the Homeric situation and Drakon's law, but in the absence of direct evidence they help support the general conclusions reached above.

---

24. If these two accounts (nos. 20, 21) are accurate, we apparently have two homicides, the first presumably intentional and the second unintentional, both leading to the purification of the killer but apparently requiring no further penalty. Probably neither Thersites nor Kephalos's wife had relatives present to demand revenge. In any case these reports, if reliable, would support the conclusion reached above, that there is no essential difference in the treatment of intentional and unintentional homicide in the epics.

25. Among the Cherokees, for instance, a homicide was avenged by the death of the killer or another member of his clan, but this death in turn brought no further retaliation; see John Phillip Reid, *A Law of Blood: The Primitive Law of the Cherokee Nation* (New York, 1970), pp. 73–84.

First, by requiring the killer's exile and also providing for pardon, at least in the case of unintentional homicide,[26] Drakon systematically combines the two main features of the epic system, exile and compensation. This suggests that these features already existed in Athens. Second, the fact that the exiled killer is explicitly protected outside Attica except in a few special places (lines 26–29) implies an earlier situation in which pursuit of the killer continued beyond the borders of the victim's own country, as is apparently the case in Homer.[27] Third, the provision of detailed regulations specifying which relatives are to decide upon pardon may indicate that uncertainty in this matter had existed previously, as is perhaps indicated by the trial scene on Achilles' shield. Moreover, the provision for retroactivity (lines 19–20), which probably applies only to these regulations, is a further indication that the regulations are new (see below, Chapter Three).

Of course we have no way of knowing how much of Drakon's law was actually created by him. We are told (*Ath. Pol.* 41.2) that Drakon was the first Athenian to write down laws; presumably he must have drawn on traditional customs to some extent, and even if we cannot say in precisely what way the treatment of homicide in Athens before Drakon was similar to what we find in the epics, the elements of the epic system form at least a plausible background for the provisions of Drakon's law.

Our historical information about pre-Drakontian

---

26. I use the term *pardon* to designate the officially sanctioned agreement between the victim's relatives and the killer which allows him to return from exile; this agreement presumably involved monetary compensation. As we shall see (below, Chap. 3), the provisions for pardon apply in most cases to both intentional and unintentional homicide.

27. Cf. Ruschenbusch, *"phonos,"* pp. 139–40.

Athens is slight, but one event has often been thought to shed light on the treatment of homicide, namely the Kylonian conspiracy, now generally dated ca. 632, or about ten years before Drakon's law.[28] One may be tempted to infer from the killing of the Kylonians and the subsequent exile of the Alkmaionids, who were primarily responsible for the killing, that exile was the regular penalty for homicide in pre-Drakontian Athens, but this argument is weakened by the fact that the killing of the Kylonians was unusual in two respects. First, however much later versions of the story may differ,[29] they all agree that some religious factor (the violation of a sanctuary or of suppliants' rights) other than the killing itself was involved, and this factor was probably primarily responsible for the Alkmaionids' pollution and exile. Second, the fact that the killing of the Kylonians was also a political act, a tyrannicide, means that it would probably be treated differently from ordinary homicides. There is thus no reason to conclude that the surviving relatives of the Kylonians must have employed the ordinary methods of obtaining revenge for homicide, nor is there any evidence that Drakon's homicide law addressed itself either to the special causes of pollution in this case or to the question of political homicide.

This does not mean that there was no connection

---

28. For the date see Stroud, p. 66, n. 7. He considers it likely that "the appointment of Drakon to draw up a code of law was a direct outcome of the Kylonian fiasco" (p. 72), and he speculates that the homicide law may have significantly hindered the Kylonians in their attempt to take vengeance for the deaths of their relatives. Sealey (pp. 98–99) is more skeptical. Edmond Levy (*Historia* 27 [1978]: 513–21) has recently revived the effort to date the conspiracy to the mid-590s. I do not find his arguments against the generally accepted date convincing.

29. The main sources are Herodotus (5.71) and Thucydides (1.126); Stroud (p. 70, n. 25) gives other references.

between the Kylonian affair and the appointment of Drakon as lawgiver in 621. The general turmoil resulting from the attempted tyranny may have helped create the demand for written laws; furthermore, if Drakon wrote a law against tyranny,[30] he could hardly have done so without the Kylonian affair in mind, if this event occurred only a few years earlier. There is, however, no reason to think that this law, if it was Drakon's, formed part of his homicide law.[31] The law against tyranny probably was directly related to the Kylonian affair; the law on homicide, as far as we can tell, was not.

If the evidence for the treatment of homicide in pre-Drakontian Athens is meager, it is no more plentiful for the history of homicide law during the two centuries separating Drakon from the Attic orators. We are told by Aristotle[32] that Solon discarded all Drakon's laws except those on homicide, and the language of the preserved fragment of the homicide law and its accompanying decree provides strong evidence that the version published in 409/8 is a more or less verbatim copy of the original law.[33] That the wording of the law was not changed even though some of it was by then obsolete should not surprise us; the conservative nature of legal language in general is well known, and Lysias (10.15–20) cites a number of examples of obsolete language in Athenian laws. Ruschenbusch has argued convincingly (*SN* 36–38), moreover, that the axones

---

30. See Ostwald, pp. 105–08.

31. This is suggested by Ostwald (p. 107), but as he himself notes (p. 108), the law against tyranny was superseded or at least supplemented by Solon's legislation, whereas the laws on homicide were retained intact.

32. *Ath. Pol.* 7.1; cf. Plut. *Sol.* 17.1 and Stroud, p. 76, n. 44 with further references.

33. See Stroud, pp. 60–64.

on which Solon's laws were inscribed survived intact at
least until the second century B.C. (more than four centuries),[34] so that the survival of Drakon's axones over half
as long a period cannot be considered unlikely.[35]

On the other hand, it has seemed incredible to many[36]
that the Athenians of the late fifth and fourth centuries
could have continued to use exactly the same homicide
laws as they did two centuries earlier. Changing social and
political institutions and the development of legal and
moral thought must have created situations with which a
seventh-century law was unable to deal, and new provisions must have been created for such situations. Such is
the implication of a passage in Antiphon (5.14 = 6.2) in
which the speaker praises the homicide laws as "the finest
and most sacred" and adds that they are "the oldest in
the land" and have remained "the same always concerning
the same matters" (τοὺς αὐτοὺς ἀεὶ περὶ τῶν αὐτῶν). The
presence of the last words (περὶ τῶν αὐτῶν) is significant
and we must not ignore them by translating simply "they

---

34. Cf. Antony Andrewes in ΦΟΡΟΣ: *Tribute to Benjamin Dean
Meritt,* ed. D. W. Bradeen and M. F. McGregor (Locust Valley, N.Y.,
1974), p. 26: "The natural conclusion from the evidence is that the
original laws of Solon were available for study in the fourth century,
and indeed much later."

35. It used to be thought that Drakon's first axon was also Solon's
first axon, but Stroud (pp. 32–34) argues convincingly that this cannot be so. His discovery of the heading "Second Axon" on our inscription has rendered the traditional view impossible, since there is
not room on the remainder of the first axon for the several other
laws that reportedly stood on Solon's first axon. On the general question of the survival of documentary evidence from the archaic period
see now R. S. Stroud, "State Documents in Archaic Athens," in
Athens Comes of Age: From Solon to Salamis (Princeton, 1978), ed.
W. A. P. Childs, pp. 20–42.

36. See, e.g., Hignett, p. 308.

have always remained unchanged," as MacDowell (p. 6)
does. Rather, Antiphon means that any particular provision
of the homicide law dealing with a specific matter has
remained unchanged, but that new provisions may have
been created concerning new situations or new aspects
of situations already covered by existing laws. We know
that the homicide laws were in fact the oldest, since Solon
repealed all Drakon's laws except these (*Ath. Pol.* 7.1),
and Antiphon's expression seems to indicate an attempt to
praise the homicide laws as highly as possible while making
no literally false statements about them.

If this is an accurate interpretation of Antiphon's expression, it suggests a simple way to account for both the
verbatim preservation of Drakon's original law in 409/8
and also the probable existence of later provisions in Athenian homicide law. We need only assume that any change
in the homicide law was made by an amendment to the law
rather than by the revision of existing provisions. Such a
theory would also explain how changes could have been
made without violating Drakon's express prohibition against
altering his law (Dem. 23.62).[37] An amendment would not
directly alter any of Drakon's original provisions, though
some amendments may in fact have modified or even ne-
gated them. Moreover, as we shall see below, some amendments included specific references to the existing law.
These amendments may have been added to the end of
Drakon's law or perhaps were published separately.[38]

---

37. There is no explicit context for the law in 23.62, but it is
probably from the homicide laws (see below, n. 49). The antiquity of
the provision is guaranteed by the word θεσμός.

38. Stroud (pp. 34, 63) suggests that Solon's amendments were
inscribed on his own axones under the appropriate official, and that
latter amendments were inscribed on a separate stele; see also Ruschenbusch, *SN*, pp. 36-37.

The revision of a set of laws by amendments that leave the text of the original provisions unchanged is common in early laws. Daube[39] has studied several examples in Hebrew law of "new provisions being joined to an existing code as an appendix instead of being worked in properly" (p. 77), and he suggests several reasons for this procedure (pp. 76–77), including the difficulty of integrating a later provision into an earlier law, the difficulty of changing a text written on stone or other material,[40] and the power of tradition. All these considerations may have affected the transmission of Drakon's homicide law.

The process of additional amendment is well illustrated in the monumental inscription of the Gortyn laws (*IC* 4.72), in which the last section (XI.24–XII.19) consists of supplementary provisions that were added at a later date, apparently by a different hand.[41] The first supplementary provision (XI.24–25) clarifies and strengthens the first section of the laws; a later supplement concerning the treatment of orphans (XII.6–19) seems to add a new element that modifies the earlier provision.[42] Both supplements apparently were added in response to situations not adequately provided for in the earlier inscription.

These considerations suggest a similar process of amendment for Drakon's law, and a law cited by Demos-

---

39. Above, n. 23, pp. 74–101.

40. Alan Boegehold (*CP* 68 [1973]:153) suggests that Drakon's original text might have been substantially altered as it was re-painted over the years, but the sort of surreptitious changes that may occasionally have been made in other sorts of texts could scarcely have been tolerated in public legal documents, and any substantial change would require a new publication.

41. See Willetts's commentary *ad loc.* The uninscribed gaps in this section of the inscription (see XI.25, 45, 55; XII.5) may indicate that each section following such a gap was added separately.

42. See Willetts, p. 27 and *ad loc.*

thenes (23.28) sheds further light on the process: τοὺς δ᾽ ἀνδροφόνους ἐξεῖναι ἀποκτείνειν ἐν τῇ ἡμεδαπῇ καὶ ἀπάγειν, ὡς ἐν τῷ ⟨α᾽⟩ ἄξονι ἀγορεύει, λυμαίνεσθαι δὲ μή, μηδὲ ἀποινᾶν, ἢ διπλοῦν ὀφείλειν ὅσον ἂν καταβλάψῃ. εἰσφέρειν δ᾽ ἐ⟨ς⟩ τοὺς ἄρχοντας, ὧν ἕκαστοι δικασταί εἰσι, τῷ βουλομένῳ. τὴν δ᾽ ἡλιαίαν διαγιγνώσκειν—"It is permissible to kill or arrest killers[43] in the territory [i.e., in Attica], as it says on the first axon,[44] but not to maltreat or ransom them, or else one shall owe twice the damages one inflicts. Anyone who wishes may lead [the violator] to the archons, whichever ones have jurisdiction over the particular crime [i.e., maltreatment or ransoming], and the Heliaia is to judge the case."[45]

It is generally accepted that Solon instituted the Heliaia as a law court,[46] and we are also told (*Ath. Pol.* 9.1) that

43. ἀνδροφόνους here probably designates convicted killers; see below, p. 59.

44. Cobet's supplement ⟨α᾽⟩ is probably correct, especially in view of Stroud's discovery that Drakon's second axon was inscribed on the surviving stele (cf. Stroud, p. 55, n. 101). Even if this emendation is not accepted, however, the argument that this is an amendment to Drakon's law remains valid, since the axon must be Drakon's in any case.

45. This last sentence is very difficult. Without Schelling's emendation δ᾽ ἐ⟨ς⟩ one must take τοὺς ἄρχοντας as the subject of εἰσφέρειν and understand "to the court," but this results in a very difficult construction for τῷ βουλομένῳ: "the archons are to present the case [to the court] for [= on behalf of?] anyone who wishes." It is easier to understand ἐξεῖναι with τῷ βουλομένῳ, in which case Schelling's emendation is necessary. This makes the expression roughly similar to what we find in Dem. 43.71: τὰς δὲ δίκας εἶναι περὶ τούτων πρὸς τοὺς ἄρχοντας ὧν ἕκαστοι δικασταί εἰσι. The reference to the archons as δικασταί attests to the antiquity of these laws; cf. Louis Gernet, *Demosthène, Plaidoyers politiques*, vol. 2 (Paris, 1959), pp. 189–90.

46. There is no evidence for the existence of the Heliaia before

he was the first to grant the power of prosecution to anyone in certain cases. Thus the law cited in Dem. 23.28 is probably not from Drakon's original law. This is also indicated by the unusual reference near the beginning of the law: ὡς ἐν τῷ ⟨αʹ⟩ ἄξονι ἀγορεύει. This reference to the "first axon" must be to Drakon's original law, where a provision allowing the killing of a convicted killer who did not go into or who returned from exile probably occupied lines 30–31.[47] If Stroud's suggested restoration of line 30 (p. 55, n. 102) is in substance correct, the original provision mentioned only the killing or arrest of a killer found in Attica. We may conclude, then, that sometime after Drakon (perhaps after someone had tried to ransom or torture a captured killer) an amendment was passed prohibiting these acts while still allowing the killing or arrest of the killer. The cross-reference to the first axon shows clearly that the original law was not revised,[48] nor was this amendment inscribed right after it, but it must have been on the second axon or later. That it was inscribed somewhere on Drakon's axones is suggested by the absence of any mention of Drakon: since Solon's laws were also inscribed on axones, the reference to the first axon (or simply "the axon") would be ambiguous unless the amendment was inscribed on or near Drakon's axones.

This brings us to a related matter, the identity of the homicide laws "from the Areopagos" (ἐξ Ἀρείου πάγου, Dem. 23.22; Lys. 1.30, 6.15). From Lysias 1.30 it appears

---

Solon; Aristotle (*Ath. Pol.* 9.1) states only that Solon created the procedure of appeal to the popular courts. Many scholars (e.g., Hignett, p. 97) assume that Solon established the Heliaia; others think he "renewed and reorganized" an existing body (Bonner and Smith, vol. 1, p. 158).

47. Stroud, pp. 54–56.
48. Stroud, p. 56.

that these laws were on a stele; whether this stood on the Areopagos or somewhere else is not known. Demosthenes apparently cites all the laws in this section of his speech against Aristocrates (23.22–82) from the laws from the Areopagos,[49] although some of them treat matters of only indirect concern to that court, since they are to be judged by other courts, such as the Heliaia (Dem. 23.28).[50] No doubt it would be important for the Areopagos to have a record of some of the relevant laws from other courts, especially laws indicating that a certain kind of homicide was not to be punished and thus was not to be tried by the Areopagos.[51]

The stele with laws from the Areopagos cannot have been the stele with Drakon's homicide law (cf. Dem. 47.71), since the latter was erected at the Stoa Basileios (lines 7–8), there is no mention of the Areopagos in the introductory decree,[52] and the first law cited by Demosthenes (23.22) could not have stood near the beginning of the surviving fragment. We might note, however, that the order of topics in the laws from the Areopagos, at least as Demosthenes presents them (see above, n. 49), is quite close to the order of the provisions on our stele: first the

---

49. The next to last law cited in the speech (23.86) is explictly said not to be from the homicide laws. This implies that all the previously cited laws were from the homicide laws, as is also implied by their content. Moreover, the expressions used to introduce each law (μετὰ ταῦτα, ἐφεξῆς, etc.) give the impression that all the laws are from one source, though these terms may simply refer to the list of laws from which the scribe is reading.

50. The term *Ephetai* in 23.37 may designate members of the Areopagos; see below, chap. 7.

51. See Lys. 1.30, where the law allowing the killing of an adulterer is said to be on the stele from the Areopagos.

52. It is possible that an exact copy of the stele at the Stoa Basileios was set up at the Areopagos.

jurisdiction of the court (23.22), then the treatments of
the unexiled killer (23.28), the exiled killer (23.37, 44),
and the returned killer (23.51), then lawful homicide
(23.53, 60), and then two other provisions (23.62, 82).
Only the law in 23.28 does not fit the order on the preserved stele.

The stele from the Areopagos thus seems to have been
a separate stele containing all the laws of more or less
direct concern to that court, including the law on intentional homicide. It is possible that this stele was first inscribed during the general re-publication and revision of
the laws in 410–03,[53] but I think it more likely that it
was inscribed earlier, perhaps when the Areopagos first
began to hear homicide cases, and was supplemented when
necessary. At any rate, the existence of such a stele is consistent with our theory that the original law of Drakon was
preserved intact and was reinscribed verbatim in 409/8,
but that a number of amendments were added to the law
in the two centuries after Drakon. Some of these amendments (such as the law in 23.28), together with some of
the original provisions of Drakon's law (such as the law in
23.37), were reinscribed on a special stele of laws from
the Areopagos.

One difficult question remains: were the amendments
to Drakon's original law also considered part of "Drakon's
law on homicide" or not? The evidence of the orators suggests that they were; Demosthenes, for instance, in 23.51
calls Drakon the author of all the homicide laws he has
cited thus far, at least one of which (23.28), as we have
seen, must be a later amendment.[54] Plutarch, on the other

---

53. For this re-publication of the laws see Stroud, pp. 21–28, with
references to earlier works.

54. The language in Dem. 23.51 (ὁ μὲν νόμος ἐστὶν οὗτος
Δράκοντος . . . καὶ οἱ ἄλλοι δὲ ὅσους ἐκ τῶν φονικῶν νόμων

hand, tells us (*Solon* 19.3) that "Drakon nowhere names the Areopagos, but in homicide matters always speaks of the Ephetai,"[55] which indicates that the law cited in Dem. 23.22 was not considered part of Drakon's law on homicide.

Plutarch's testimony is probably the more reliable, since he is reporting on a scholarly dispute, and if the claim were not true it could easily have been disproved by someone in the opposing camp. The remarks of the orators, on the other hand, are often unreliable, though Demosthenes' statement does indicate that it was plausible to treat all these laws on the stele from the Areopagos as part of Drakon's law. Faced with this contradictory evidence, we may conclude that the amendments, though perhaps inscribed on the same axones and stele as Drakon's original law, were kept separate from the original text of the law; however, they could be and often were treated simply as part of Drakon's homicide law.

In any case, the theory of change by amendment is a plausible hypothesis and provides the only satisfactory way of accounting for the preservation of Drakon's law in its original form in the fifth and fourth centuries together with other provisions of the homicide law which cannot have been in the original law. By the fourth century certain provisions of the original law were obsolete, others may have been superseded in parts, and new details had certainly been added, but the basic provisions of Drakon's original law were still valid.

παρεγραψάμην) is perhaps imprecise enough to allow the conclusion that Demosthenes does not mean to include among the φονικοὶ νόμοι all the laws he has previously cited, and thus does not in fact think the law in 23.28 is Drakon's.

55. On the difficult question of the relation between these two bodies and the evidence of Plutarch, *Sol.* 19, see below, chap. 7.

CHAPTER THREE

THE PROVISIONS OF DRAKON'S LAW

We now turn to the law itself as preserved on the stele inscribed in 409/8. I shall discuss each of the surviving provisions in order before turning in Chapter Four to the most controversial issue: where and what was the law on intentional homicide?

LINE 11

The law as preserved begins with a provision setting exile as the penalty for unintentional homicide: καὶ ἐὰν μὴ ἐκ προνοίας [κ] τ[είνῃ τίς τινα, φεύγ] ει[ν].[1] Probably the most controversial word in the law is the initial καί; because the interpretation of its meaning and function is of crucial importance for the dispute concerning the law on inten-

---

1. The restoration of this clause has recently been disputed by K. Tsantsanoglou (ΚΕΡΝΟΣ [Thessalonika, 1972], pp. 170–79, 250), who reads καὶ ἐὰν μὴ ἐκ προνοίας κτείνῃ τις, φόνου φεύγειν: "Even if someone does not intentionally kill, he shall stand trial for homicide." But none of Tsantsanoglou's objections to the traditional restoration are convincing, and his own reading would mean that Drakon discussed pardon in homicide cases without having mentioned the penalty for homicide, which seems unlikely. Note that one of his reasons for rejecting the traditional restoration is that "καὶ ἐάν has a concessive force ('even if') which would lead to the inadmissible inference that exile was also the regular punishment for intentional murderers" (p. 250). I shall show (below, chap. 7) that this inference is perfectly admissible.

tional homicide, I shall postpone discussion of καί and ignore it for the moment. The other controversial matter in this line is the sense of πρόνοια. The expression μὴ ἐκ προνοίας has been rendered in English as "without premeditation," "not deliberately," "unintentionally," or "involuntarily," with similar variations in other languages. Although some authors seem to use these terms almost interchangeably, there are important differences among them, and we must try to determine as precisely as possible what Drakon understood by ἐκ προνοίας and its negation. In particular we must ask whether Drakon distinguished between homicide committed μὴ ἐκ προνοίας and homicide committed ἄκων (ἀκούσιος), or whether these two expressions were for practical purposes interchangeable. The same question arises with respect to ἐκ προνοίας and ἑκών (ἑκούσιος).

Although there has been much dispute concerning the precise sense of πρόνοια, there is general agreement that ἑκών and ἐκ προνοίας are roughly equivalent. Gernet concludes that "la comparaison des textes affirme que ἑκών et ἐκ προνοίας s'emploient l'un pour l'autre, et que l'expression assez frequent de ἑκών ἐκ προνοίας n'est qu'un redoublement,"[2] and Maschke (pp. 42–53) concurs, at least with respect to Drakon's law. But Maschke sees a change in the sense of πρόνοια by the age of the orators (pp. 53–63), when in his view ἐκ προνοίας means "premeditated" (überlegt), and he thus assumes a distinction in the later period between ἑκών and ἐκ προνοίας and also between ἄκων and μὴ ἐκ προνοίας. Maschke concludes that although μὴ ἐκ προνοίας and ἄκων are used synonymously in Drakon's law, the former includes intentional but unpremeditated homicide (Totschlag, second-degree

---

2. Louis Gernet, *Recherches sur le développement de la pensée juridique et morale en Grèce* (Paris, 1917), p. 352.

murder),[3] whereas the latter is normally limited to unintentional homicide (*unvorsätzliche Tötung,* roughly equivalent
to involuntary manslaughter).
Stroud similarly translates πρόνοια "premeditation"
and suggests (pp. 40–41) the possibility that μὴ ἐκ προνοίας
in Drakon's law may include intentional but unpremeditated homicide as distinct from ἄκων, which designates
only unintentional homicide. Taking up Stroud's cautious
suggestion, Cantarella (pp. 95–106) has recently argued
vigorously that in Drakon's law μὴ ἐκ προνοίας and ἄκων
must be different. She maintains that there are two separate categories of unpremeditated homicide, φόνος μὴ ἐκ
προνοίας (*l'omicidio non premeditato,* second-degree
murder) and φόνος ἀκούσιος (*l'omicidio colposo,* also
roughly equivalent to involuntary manslaughter), but only
one category of premeditated homicide. Cantarella concludes that Drakon's law recognized three categories of
intent: ἐκών (= ἐκ προνοίας), μὴ ἐκ προνοίας, and ἄκων.
Many of the arguments of these scholars are based on
selected passages in Homer and the orators which do not
in fact support their conclusions. For example, both
Maschke (pp. 5–9) and Cantarella (pp. 43–49) discuss
Patroklos's killing of his playmate in anger (χολωθείς) but
οὐκ ἐθέλων (*Il.* 23.87–88), and both consider this killing
unintentional (ἄκων). It seems clear, however, that at least
in classical times killing a person by striking a blow in
anger in a quarrel was considered intentional homicide
even if one did not intend to kill,[4] and we must thus
reject the conclusion that Patroklos's homicide would have
been considered unintentional.[5]

---

3. For these categories of homicide in American law see above,
chap. 1.
4. Cf. Ant. 4.3.4.
5. See above, chap. 2, n. 13. Naturally the retrospective dis-

We must be extremely cautious, moreover, about the use of logical deductions in analyzing these terms. For example, the fact—if it is a fact, as Cantarella (pp 98–101) maintains, and not simply rhetorical exaggeration—that the expression τραῦμα ἐκ προνοίας in Lysias 3 and 4 designates "wounding with intent to kill" does not prove that φόνος ἐκ προνοίας must mean "homicide committed with intent to kill." As Holmes wrote, "The life of the law has not been logic, it has been experience," and inconsistencies in legal terminology are by no means unknown.[6] Furthermore, even if it is shown that ἐκ προνοίας in some cases (e.g., Ant. 1) refers to a premeditated homicide, this does not mean that the general category of φόνος ἐκ προνοίας must be limited to such homicide. Rather, we must look at the overall usage of the orators and others to see precisely how the terms are used in legal contexts, particularly in the context of homicide.

Much of the evidence has recently been examined by Loomis[7] in an effort to determine the precise meaning of πρόνοια (which he generally translates "premeditation"). Loomis first considers the extent to which ἐκ προνοίας and ἑκών (ἑκούσιος) on the one hand and μὴ ἐκ προνοίας and ἄκων (ἀκούσιος) on the other overlap, and he concludes (p. 90) that although πρόνοια means more than ἑκών, ἑκών and ἐκ προνοίας have the same legal force, and similarly

avowal of intent in such cases cannot be considered an objective statement; cf. Theseus's similar disavowal in Eur. *Hipp.* 1433–34.

6. Oliver Wendell Holmes, *The Common Law* (Boston, 1881), p. 1. In Lecture Two Holmes discusses (among other things) "malice" and shows (p. 45) that "malice, in the definition of murder, has not the same meaning as in common speech," and (p. 52) that in other statutes which use the expression "wilfully and maliciously" malice "has nothing in common with the malice of murder."

7. *JHS* 92 (1972):86–95.

ἄκων and μὴ ἐκ προνοίας are legally equivalent. Loomis
concludes also (p. 94) that πρόνοια is equivalent to "intent"
and that in homicide cases the intent need not be to kill
but only to harm: "I suppose, therefore, that the most
accurate translation of πρόνοια, at least in the context of
homicide, would be 'harmful intent.'"

I agree with Loomis that this is the sense of πρόνοια in
homicide cases[8] and that "the practical effect of this was
to narrow unintentional homicides to our category of
accidental killings."[9] These conclusions are supported by
a passage from [Aristotle's] *Magna Moralia* (1188B29–
38),[10] where the nature of an unintentional act (ἄκοντα
ποιῆσαι) is illustrated by the case of a woman acquitted
of homicide (by poison) because she thought she was
administering a love potion and thus acted οὐκ ἐκ προνοίας.
This expression must mean "not intentionally," since
the question here is not one of deliberation or premeditation but of intent, and the jury decided that she gave the
potion to the victim φιλίᾳ, i.e., with no intent to harm.[11]
The passage demonstrates well that as legal expressions
οὐκ ἐκ προνοίας, οὐχ ἑκούσιος, and ἄκων are virtually equivalent.

There are, moreover, a number of other passages in
the orators where a clear opposition is presented between
ἄκων/ἀκούσιος and ἑκών/ἑκούσιος,[12] between ἄκων and

---

8. The best evidence is the case of Konon and Ariston (Dem.
54.25–28), discussed by Loomis, pp. 92–93.

9. Ibid., p. 93. It is regrettable that Loomis's language frequently
implies that our categories are the norm from which the Greeks
deviated.

10. The passage from the *Magna Moralia* is ignored by Cantarella
but is cited by MacDowell (p. 46) and Loomis (p. 89).

11. MacDowell's translation of πρόνοια and διάνοια in this passage
as "deliberation" (followed by Loomis) is misleading.

12. E.g., Ant. 5.92: τὰ μὲν ἀκούσια τῶν ἁμαρτημάτων ἔχει

ἐκ προνοίας,[13] and between ἄκων and ἑκὼν ἐκ προνοίας.[14] It is clear from these passages and from the absence of any evidence to the contrary that in legal matters the Greeks normally recognized only two categories of action, intentional and unintentional, and two passages in Demosthenes (21.43, 23.45–49) make this conclusion especially certain with respect to homicide. Moreover, we know from Aristotle (*Ath. Pol.* 57.3; see also Dem. 23.65–73) that the Athenian homicide courts recognized only two degrees of punishable homicide, intentional (tried at the Areopagos) and unintentional (tried at the Palladion).

There is no trace anywhere in the orators or in Athenian law of a third category between ἄκων and ἑκὼν/ἐκ προνοίας. When Plato (*Laws* 866D–869E) describes an intermediate category of homicide, killing in anger (θυμῷ), he is introducing his own innovation, and Aristotle begins his discussion of intentional action in the *Nicomachean Ethics* (3.1) with the basic distinction between τὸ ἑκούσιον and τὸ ἀκούσιον, though he goes on to make further distinctions within these two categories. Cantarella argues entirely from the supposed meanings of πρόνοια and ἄκων by themselves that οὐ/μὴ ἐκ προνοίας must be different from ἄκων, but she can present no direct evidence (except the alleged evidence of Drakon's law) for a category of φόνος οὐ/μὴ ἐκ προνοίας separate from φόνος ἀκούσιος.

In fact the expression οὐ/μὴ ἐκ προνοίας probably does

συγγνώμην, τὰ δὲ ἑκούσια οὐκ ἔχει. τὸ μὲν γὰρ ἀκούσιον ἁμάρτημα τῆς τύχης ἐστί, τὸ δὲ ἑκούσιον τῆς γνώμης. Cf. Ant. 3 passim; Lys. 13.28; Dem. 18.274, 21.43, 23.47, 23.48; and Herod. 2.65.5.

13. E.g., Dem. 21.43: οἱ φονικοὶ [*sc.* νόμοι] τοὺς μὲν ἐκ προνοίας ἀποκτιννύντας . . . ζημιοῦσι, τοὺς δ' ἀκουσίως αἰδέσεως . . . ἠξίωσαν; cf. 23.45, 23.50.

14. E.g., Ant. 1.27: ἐλεεῖν ἐπὶ τοῖς ἀκουσίοις παθήμασι μᾶλλον προσήκει ἢ τοῖς ἑκουσίοις καὶ ἐκ προνοίας ἀδικήμασι καὶ ἁμαρτήμασι; cf. 1.5.

not designate any specific category of homicide but is used
merely to negate ἐκ προνοίας, much as one might say in
English, "It was not premeditated homicide," where the
expression designates no single other category (though
in a specific context it might be virtually equivalent to
"unpremeditated homicide"). In other words, the few
times the expression οὐ/μὴ ἐκ προνοίας occurs, its effect
is to deny that a particular action belongs to the category ἐκ προνοίας. Apart from Drakon's law I have found
only five occurrences in the major classical prose authors
(Herod., Thuc,. Xen., the orators, Plato, Arist.) of the
expression οὐ/μὴ ἐκ προνοίας,[15] and in every case it negates
a positive category and we should translate it "not intentionally" rather than "unintentionally." This observation
has important consequences for our understanding of the
first line of Drakon's law (see below, p. 103), which I shall
translate (omitting καί) "If a man not intentionally kills
another, he is exiled."

     In sum, there existed in Athenian homicide law only
two categories of intent, which I designate "intentional"
and "unintentional." The terms ἐκ προνοίας and ἑκών
(ἑκούσιος) or both are used for the former, the term ἄκων
(ἀκούσιος) for the latter.[16] The difference between ἑκών
and ἐκ προνοίας is one of emphasis: the latter is the stronger

---

     15. Herod. 1.120.3: μὴ ἐκ προνοίης τινός (where τινός makes
the effect clear—"not from any πρόνοια"); Ant. 6.19: μὴ ἐκ προνοίας
μηδ' ἐκ παρασκευῆς; Ais. 3.178: ἐξ ἔθους ἀλλ' οὐκ ἐκ προνοίας;
(4) [Arist.] MM 1188B35: διότι οὐκ ἐκ προνοίας . . . διὸ οὐχ ἑκούσιον
. . . οὐ μετὰ διανοίας; (5) [Arist.] Problems 952A2: ἔτι μείζω μὲν
ἀδικεῖ ὁ ἐκ προνοίας ἀδικῶν ἢ ὁ μὴ ἐκ προνοίας.
     16. Later discussions of the homicide courts (e.g., Ailian VH
5.15, Hellad. apud Photios Bibl. 535A22–26; cf. Arist. Pol. 1300B25–
26) regularly refer to the Areopagos as the court for homicide ἐκ
προνοίας and the Palladion as the court for homicide ἄκων (ἀκούσιος).

term and is used to stress the intentional nature of an act; for extra emphasis both terms are used together.

LINES 11–13

The second provision of the law contains a gap of seventeen letters that we cannot restore with certainty:[17] δικάζειν δὲ τοὺς βασιλέας αἴτιο[ν] (αἰτίων?) φόν[ου] E . . . Ε [β]ουλεύσαντα· τοὺς δὲ ἐφέτας διαγνῶναι. The traditional supplement is based on the interpretation of the text as αἰτίων: δικάζειν δὲ τοὺς βασιλέας αἰτίων φόνου [ἢ ἐάν τις αἰτιᾶται ὡς][18] βουλεύσαντα, which is said to mean either "the kings[19] are to decide on the causes of the homicide or if a man accuses [another] of planning [a homicide]" or "the kings are to judge accusations of homicide or if a man accuses [another] of planning [a homicide]." Whichever meaning one chooses, there are considerable difficulties: δικάζειν with a genitive of this sort is unparalleled;[20] αἰτία in either of these senses

---

17. For a good discussion of the problem of supplementing line 12 see Stroud, pp. 43–45, 47. He includes some of the arguments I make against the traditional supplement. MacDowell (pp. 118–19) adheres to the traditional supplement.

18. The traditional supplement would have to be altered, of course, to fit Stroud's new letters.

19. For the plural see below, pp. 46–47.

20. See Stroud, p. 43, n. 48. The usual parallel cited for δικάζειν αἰτίων in the sense of "judge accusations" is δικάζουσι ἐγκλήματος (Xen. Cyr. 1.2.7). But an examination of the context of this expression reveals that the noun which really completes δικάζουσι here is ἀχαριστίας [sc. δίκην], in apposition to and anticipated by ἐγκλήματος: δικάζουσι δὲ καὶ ἐγκλήματος οὗ ἕνεκα ἄνθρωποι μισοῦσι μὲν ἀλλήλους μάλιστα, δικάζονται δὲ ἥκιστα, ἀχαριστίας. In the simple phrase δικάζειν ἀχαριστίας, however, ἐγκλήματος would be meaningless, just as αἰτίων would be a meaningless addition to

does not otherwise predate the fifth century;[21] moreover, either the conditional clause is very awkwardly placed if it is assumed to be syntactically parallel to the opening protasis,[22] or else a crucial element is missing, namely, a specific indication of the penalty for planning a homicide.[23] A final difficulty is that the traditional supplement does not fit the new epsilon Stroud discovered in the forty-seventh stoichos of line 12.

A different approach to the problem, suggested by several earlier scholars, was persuasively argued by Wolff (pp. 71–73), who raised several of the objections mentioned above to the reading αἰτίων and defended the alternate interpretation of the text, αἴτιον. Wolff proposed the supplement δικάζειν δὲ τοὺς βασιλέας αἴτιον φόνου [ἢ τὸν αὐτόχειρα ἢ τὸν] βουλεύσαντα, which yields the sense "the kings are to adjudge responsible for homicide either the actual killer or the planner [of a homicide]"; and both Ruschenbusch and Stroud have accepted Wolff's view, though each proposes a slightly different restoration.[24] Wolff's supplement produces exactly the required sense:

---

the phrase δικάζειν φόνου. I have seen no parallel suggested for δικάζειν αἰτίων in the sense of "decide on the cause."

21. LSJ gives Pindar O. 1.35 as the earliest occurrence of αἰτία.

22. Bonner and Smith (1:113) simply transpose the clause in their translation: "If anyone kills a man without premeditation or if anyone is charged with plotting homicide, he shall be exiled. . . ." A further difficulty with this solution is that exile apparently would be the penalty for those who are merely accused of planning a homicide. Cantarella (pp. 93–94) revives Maschke's suggestion (see below, n. 34) that the clause ἢ ἐάν . . . βουλεύσαντα is a later interpolation.

23. The reader must supply the rest of the thought himself: "or if a man accuses another of planning [a homicide, the kings are to consider this equivalent to a cause/accusation of homicide]."

24. Ruschenbusch (SN F5a): αἴτιον φόνου εἶ [ναι ἢ χειρὶ

the responsibility for a homicide lies equally on the planner and he will thus be subject to the same treatment as the actual killer. This also eliminates the difficulty with αἰτία, since αἴτιος in this sense is common in Homer and even occurs in Drakon's law itself (lines 23–24, 27).[25] The difficulties which remain are, first, that δικάζειν in this sense does not elsewhere take an accusative of the person judged,[26] and second, that Wolff's supplement does not fit the new letters Stroud has found. Both these difficulties could be eliminated by reading, e.g., δικάζειν δὲ τοὺς βασιλέας αἴτιον φόνου εἴ [ναι τὸν ἐργασάμενον] ἢ βουλεύσαντα.[27] Other supplements are certainly possible,[28] but

---

κτείναντα ἢ βου]λεύσαντα; Stroud (p. 47): αἴτιον φόνου ε[ἴτε τὸν αὐτόχειρα εἴτ]ε [β]ουλεύσαντα.

25. There may be an inconsistency between the sense of αἴτιος φόνου in line 12, where it includes the killer as well as the planner, and in line 27, where it does not (ἐάν τις ... κτείνῃ ἢ αἴτιος ᾖ φόνου), but I do not consider this a serious difficulty (see Wolff, p. 73, n. 186). One could use the English expression "responsible for a homicide" in both places with no sense of inconsistency.

26. Before the fifth century δικάζειν is usually used absolutely, and otherwise takes only a cognate accusative, δίκην (e.g., Hes. WD 39, fr. 338; Theognis 543–44). Later δικάζειν may take an accusative of the dispute or the crime being judged or the penalty being determined.

27. For ἐργασάμενον see And. 1.94; both Paoli (cited by Ruschenbusch, SN F5a) and Tsantsanoglou (above, n. 1) have suggested restorations using ἐργασάμενον. δικάζειν is used with the infinitive several times in the Gortyn laws, usually in the aorist (I.6, I.28–29, III.6, V.31; cf. IC 4.47.17–18, etc.). H. Jacobsthal, Der Gebrauch der Tempora und Modi in den kretischen Dialektin-schriften (Strassburg, 1907), pp. 38–43, maintains that only the aorist is used with an infinitive, but his attempt to remove the one stumbling block to this hypothesis (IX.38–40) is unconvincing.

28. See above, nn. 24 and 27.

any reconstruction along the lines set down by Wolff will produce essentially the same sense: "The kings are to adjudge responsible[29] for homicide either the actual killer or the planner [of a homicide]; and the Ephetai are to judge the case."

At first glance the meaning of this provision seems clear: the planner of a homicide is to be considered responsible for the killing and is to be subject to the same legal procedure as one who actually carries out the deed. This was a well-established rule of Athenian homicide law, as we know from Andocides 1.94 (τὸν βουλεύσαντα ἐν τῷ αὐτῷ ἐνέχεσθαι[30] καὶ τὸν τῇ χειρὶ ἐργασάμενον),[31] and it is possible that it was an established custom before Drakon.[32] It is not surprising that the rule comes early in the law, for it is an important provision; without it, for instance, a person could effectively kill with impunity simply by hiring the services of others. This interpretation raises a serious difficulty, however, since the provision occurs in a context which has suggested to many that its application is restricted to cases of unintentional homicide. We must thus consider what might be meant by βουλεύω

---

29. I use "responsible" in the sense of "legally liable." For my reservations about "responsible" as a translation of αἴτιος, see Gagarin, *Drama*, esp. pp. 6–7 and 168, n. 28.

30. The expression ἐνέχεσθαι ἐν is usually used with a dative indicating a penalty, a charge, or a law (see LSJ s.v. ἐνέχω II.b). When it occurs with an unspecified τῷ αὐτῷ, as here, it seems to indicate that the treatment is the same in all respects.

31. This principle is introduced by the statement οὗτος ὁ νόμος καὶ πρότερον ἦν καὶ ὡς καλῶς ἔχων καὶ νῦν ἔστι καὶ χρῆσθε αὐτῷ. Andokides is maintaining that an informer is responsible for the death of someone he denounces. Cf. Ant. 4.2.5.

32. This seems to be implied by the death of Klytaimestra; see above, chap. 2.

in the context of unintentional homicide. Can one "plan" an unintentional homicide?[33]

It is clear that the basic sense of βουλεύω is "take counsel, deliberate" and then "plan, devise," whether one carries out the plan oneself or entrusts it to another.[34] The evidence from the Homeric poems and other early literature is not sufficient to enable us to determine exactly how involved in a homicide a person had to be in order to be accused of planning it; nor must we necessarily accept Maschke's claim (p. 89) that the category αἴτιος φόνου was necessarily broader than that of βουλεύσας τὸν φόνον.[35] It is clear, however, that in Homer βουλεύω always refers to conscious intellectual activity, and with one exception (see below) I know of no example where it might be used with reference to an unintentional deed. Plato, for instance, distinguishes (Laws 872A1) one who "plans" (βουλεύσῃ) an intentional homicide from the αὐτόχειρ (cf. 872B5), but with respect to unintentional homicide he mentions only a death occurring "through the agency of others" (δι᾽ ἑτέρων σωμάτων, 865C1).

---

33. Many difficult problems arise in connection with this matter of bouleusis (as it is called) of unintentional homicide. Here I can only treat briefly a few issues of particular significance for Drakon's law. I hope to treat the whole question more fully in a separate study.

34. The most thorough study of βουλεύω is Maschke's (pp. 83–92). His view that Drakon's law is heavily interpolated makes his study less useful for us, especially since he considers the reference to the βουλεύσαντα in lines 12–13 to be one of the later interpolations. See also Wolff, pp. 72–73.

35. Strictly speaking, αἴτιος φόνου must include one who actually strikes the blow, as apparently it does in line 12. In line 27, however, it apparently designates one who did not himself kill but who is otherwise responsible; see above, n. 25.

This fact should not surprise us; certainly in English
the expression "planning an unintentional act" is, in the
ordinary use of these words, a contradiction in terms.[36]
Indeed, it is perhaps more surprising to come across even
one example of βουλεύω used of an unintentional act,
but such is apparently the case in Antiphon 6. According
to the speaker, his accusers have charged him with the
homicide[37] (by poison) of a young chorus boy by reason
of his having planned the death (ἀποκτεῖναί με . . .
βουλεύσαντα τὸν θάνατον, 6.16).[38] They have also agreed,
however, that the death was unintentional (ὁμολογοῦσι
μὴ ἐκ προνοίας μηδ᾽ ἐκ παρασκευῆς γενέσθαι τὸν θάνατον,
6.19). If we assume that the speaker is accurately representing the accusation against him,[39] how are we to

---

36. This consideration led H. J. Treston (*Poine: A Study in
Ancient Greek Blood-Vengeance* [London, 1923], p. 195) to suggest that the gap in line 12 be supplemented with [. . . μὴ
βου]λεύσαντα, but this has found no support.

37. *Pace* MacDowell (pp. 63–64), the defendant in this case is
charged with homicide (φόνου δίκην, 6.36) not *bouleusis,* as is clear
from the prosecutor's oath that the defendant killed the boy and
the defendant's own assertion that he did not kill him either with
his own hand or by planning (6.16): διωμόσαντο δὲ οὗτοι μὲν
ἀποκτεῖναί με Διόδοτον βουλεύσαντα τὸν θάνατον, ἐγὼ δὲ μὴ
ἀποκτεῖναι, μήτε χειρὶ ἐργασάμενος [mss.: ἀράμενος] μήτε βουλεύσας.

38. The fact that the charge is unintentional homicide may
explain why the expression βουλεύσαντα τὸν θάνατον is used rather
than βουλεύσαντα τὸν φόνον, since φόνος might imply intentional
homicide; see below, pp. 105–07.

39. Such an assumption is always risky, but here the reference
to the prosecution's oath (6.16) makes it more likely that their
words are being accurately quoted. In 6.19, however, ὁμολογοῦσι
may indicate that the speaker is only paraphrasing or drawing an
inference from his accuser's argument, and on this evidence alone
we cannot completely rule out the possibility that the accuser had

interpret this charge of "planning" an unintentional homicide? What precise activity was he accused of?

The defendant's argument seems to confirm that he was not charged with carrying out the homicide with his own hand, for he emphatically denies four different acts (6.15-17): he neither ordered the boy to drink the potion, nor compelled him, nor gave it to him to drink, nor was he even present when the boy drank. He tells us that although he was the choregos he had delegated the training of the chorus to others, and we may assume that one or more of these assistants was the direct cause of the boy's drinking the potion. Moreover, if the prosecution did in fact agree that the death was unintentional, we must suppose that the potion was not intended to harm the boy; most likely it was intended to help his voice.

Beyond his specific denial, the defendant's speech is notably deficient in facts. He never tells us what in fact he did do or how the death occurred; he blames only fate (6.15). He gives no indication, moreover, that the prosecution's speech was any more specific,[40] and he implies by the language he uses in a series of hypothetical denials ("If they say that one who orders does wrong, then I did no wrong, for I did not order," etc., 6.17) that the pros-

---

brought a charge of intentional homicide. The defendant, however, is almost certainly telling the truth, since the charge would have been clear to anyone because of the court at which the case was being tried—either the Areopagos (intentional homicide) or the Palladion (unintentional homicide).

40. In 6.21 the speaker says the victim's brother accused him at the Heliaia of having killed the boy φάρμακον ἀναγκάσας πιεῖν. Even if this is true, it does not mean that this specific charge was included in the accusation in this case. The accusation before the Heliaia was probably made in connection with the speaker's suits against his enemies in a separate case.

ecution was not more specific in its charge than simply
βουλεύσαντα τὸν θάνατον.[41] Most of the defendant's speech
concerns the events after the death, the special motives
his enemies have for wanting him prosecuted, and the
means by which they induced the victim's relatives to prosecute him. If we accept the defendant's story, at least in
its general outline, the following picture emerges.

The defendant as choregos had delegated the training
of the chorus to several assistants. When one boy needed
a drug for his voice, the assistants provided it to him; it
proved fatal. The assistants may have consulted with the
choregos about this; the prosecution would probably
claim that they did in any case, though they would have a
difficult time proving such a claim. No one else seems to
have been prosecuted for the homicide,[42] but immediately
after the funeral the choregos's political enemies persuaded
(bribed?) the boy's brother to bring a homicide suit against
the choregos. Their intention was to force him to drop the
suits he was bringing against them in other cases, since anyone who stood accused of homicide could not engage in
other legal affairs.[43]

If the prosecution's primary concern was simply to
bring a homicide suit against the choregos regardless of its

---

41. The defendant would probably feel compelled to answer a
specific accusation with a specific response, but we cannot be certain
that the lack of a response means there was no accusation. In 6.7–8
the speaker claims that his accusers devoted most of their speech to
slandering him for his other activities, which seems plausible.

42. If anyone else had been prosecuted for homicide, the defendant presumably would have mentioned the fact in 6.15. The person
who actually gave the drug would be liable for a charge of unintentional homicide, but perhaps the prosecution of the choregos in this
case was considered sufficient.

43. ὁ νόμος οὕτως ἔχει, ἐπειδάν τις ἀπογραφῇ φόνου δίκην,
εἴργεσθαι τῶν νομίμων (Ant. 6.36).

chances of success, then it would not matter that they could charge him only with an unspecified involvement in the death. They labeled this involvement βουλεύσαντα τὸν θάνατον and prosecuted him for unintentional homicide on the ground that the planner of a homicide is just as responsible as the actual killer. Since this rule was well established and was not explicitly limited to intentional homicide (though this surely was its usual application, as in And. 1.94), a charge of planning an unintentional homicide would be technically possible even if it was an apparent contradiction in terms.

On the basis of this interpretation of the case in Antiphon 6, I suggest that the use of βουλεύω in connection with a charge of unintentional homicide must have developed in several stages: first, the general rule was recognized that someone who plans a homicide (needless to say, an intentional homicide) is as responsible as the person who carries out the plan. Second, this principle was incorporated into a written homicide law; at this stage there was no mention of intent since βουλεύω implies intentional homicide and no need was felt explicitly to exclude unintentional homicide. Third, at a later date this law was applied to a case of unintentional homicide, as in Antiphon 6. Cases of "planning an unintentional homicide" were undoubtedly rare, and this special application did not affect the normal usage of βουλεύω (see above on Plato's *Laws*).

We must thus conclude that the use of βουλεύω in Antiphon 6 in connection with an unintentional homicide is abnormal, and this case cannot affect our understanding of the term in Drakon's law, where it must designate intentional homicide even though it is not explicitly limited to this category. The clause in lines 11–13 declaring both the killer and the planner responsible for a homicide is thus a general statement of a legal principle whose application was normally assumed to extend only to intentional

homicide. The possibility that the clause could apply to
unintentional homicide probably occurred to no one at
this time, and thus intent is not specifically mentioned.
Drakon's purpose was simply to include planners of homicides along with actual killers in the provisions of his
homicide law.

This provision raises two further questions: who are
the basileis? and what precise function is designated by
δικάζειν? In classical times the basileus (or archon basileus)
had general supervision of all homicide cases. He accepted
the plaintiff's case, heard preliminary evidence, assigned
the case to one of the courts, and so forth. It is a plausible
assumption that he also performed these functions in
Drakon's time. The difficulty is that after the establishment
of the archon system at Athens (well before Drakon's
time) there was only one basileus annually. Thus the plural
in Drakon's law[44] has troubled scholars, and two different
explanations have been suggested.[45]

One is that the basileis are the archon basileus and the
four phylobasileis who in classical times presided at the
Prytaneion. Though in the fourth century the phylobasileis
apparently did not preside at any of the courts where the
Ephetai were jurors, we know virtually nothing of their
functions in Drakon's time, and it is possible that they are
designated, together with the archon basileus, by the
plural in Drakon's law. It is also possible that Drakon uses
the plural to designate either the basileus, who would
preside in a case where a killer is named, or the phylobasileis, who would pronounce the unknown killer guilty at
the Prytaneion.

The other explanation, favored by Stroud, is that the

---

44. The plural also occurs in Solon's amnesty decree (Plut. *Sol.*
19.4), for which see below, pp. 128–32.
45. See Stroud, pp. 45–47 for references to earlier views.

plural refers to the archon basileus in successive years. This strikes me as very unlikely: the plural would be abnormal as well as unnecessary, and the parallels cited are not convincing.[46] Thus I find the first solution preferable, though it is perhaps best, with MacDowell (pp. 87–88), to leave the question open.

The activity of these kings, δικάζειν, is distinguished from that of the Ephetai, διαγνῶναι (line 13; cf. line 29).[47] If the difference between these two verbs is the same as that between δικάζειν and κρίνειν in the Gortyn laws,[48] then the former designates the pronouncing of a verdict when the procedure is such that the judge has no choice in the matter, whereas the latter designates the actual making of a decision based on the evidence.[49] In effect the Ephetai were the jury who decided the case, and the basileus (or basileis) the judge who pronounced the verdict. If the killer immediately went into exile, then a trial was

---

46. In both examples commonly cited (*IG* II².1174; *RIG* 998.46–47) there is a generally plural context, which accounts for the plural references to successive officials. This is true neither for Drakon's law nor for Solon's amnesty decree. To my knowledge no other parallel has been adduced.

47. It is hard to see why δικάζειν is a present infinitive and διαγνῶναι aorist. It is possible that the act of pronouncing a man guilty was thought to persist in its effects whereas the judicial decision was seen as a momentary act. Whatever the explanation, the use of the present, διαγιγνώσκειν, in lines 29 (but see below, n. 78) and (apparently) 35 is difficult to account for. In the Gortyn laws there is no apparent reason for the variation between present and aorist of καταδικάζειν (I.4, I.8) or κρίνειν (V.43–44, VI.54, XI.30), though Jacobsthal (above, n. 27, pp. 141–42) suggests a possible reason for the latter case.

48. See J. W. Headlam, *JHS* 13 (1892):48–69, and Wolff, pp. 75–76; cf. Harrison, vol. 2, p. 38, n. 1.

49. For διαγιγνώσκειν in this sense see, e.g., Ant. 6.3, Lys. 7.22.

probably unnecessary and the judge simply pronounced a
verdict of guilty. If the killer (or his relatives) contested
the charge of homicide, then the Ephetai would have to
decide the case.

This sense of δικάζειν is narrower than its common
meaning in Homer and Hesiod, where it is used to designate
the formal or informal settling of disputes. [50] We may
speculate that it acquired this narrower sense from its connection with the basileis who decide disputes in Hesiod
(*WD* 39). [51] Later, with the institution of a special body to
decide disputed cases, the power of the basileus was
restricted to pronouncing the verdict, but this activity continued to be designated by the traditional verb associated
with the office of basileus.

LINES 13-19

The next portion of the law states the regulations concerning pardon. [52] Those relatives who may grant pardon are
divided into two categories and a further provision is added

---

50. *Il.* 1.542, 8.431, 23.574; *Od.* 11.547; Hes. *WD* 39, fr. 43a.38.

51. See Louis Gernet, *L'année sociologique*, 3d ser. (1948-49),
pp. 101-102 (= *Anthropologie de la Grèce antique* [Paris, 1968],
pp. 244-45).

52. Martin Ostwald has made me aware that "pardon" is an
inadequate translation for αἰδέσασθαι, which means "respect the
person of." Originally it probably designated a purely private
reconciliation between the killer and the victim's relatives, but in
Drakon's law this private reconciliation is publicly recognized and
sanctioned, and in the fourth century αἴδεσις as a legal term is
fully equivalent to "pardon" (Dem. 21.43, *Ath. Pol.* 57.3, and for
αἰδέσεσθαι Dem. 23.77, 37.59, etc.). I shall also use *pardon* to
designate the readmission (ἐσέσθων, line 18) of the exiled killer to
the city by ten phratry members, since these two activities are by
implication legally equivalent. Cf. Glotz, pp. 94-103.

in case no relatives are still living: "If there is a father or brother or sons, pardon is to be agreed to by all, or the one who opposes is to prevail; but if none of these survives, by those up to the degree of first cousin once removed and first cousin,[53] if all are willing to agree to a pardon; the one who opposes is to prevail;[54] but if not one of these survives, and if he killed unintentionally (ἄκων) and the fifty-one, the Ephetai, decide he killed unintentionally (ἄκοντα), let ten phratry members admit him [to the country] and let the fifty-one choose these by rank."

The law does not state precisely when or how agreement on pardon is to be reached, but certain inferences may be drawn. If we begin with the third case, where no relatives survive, we may infer that admission to the country would take place only after the killer has been convicted and gone into exile. This inference is supported by the stipulation that the homicide must be judged uninten-

---

53. For these degrees of relationship see MacDowell, p. 18.

54. Stroud's new letters in line 16 have happily eliminated the traditional restoration, which introduced an oath for the relatives, but his restoration of lines 14–16 has produced an anomalous asyndeton: [ἐὰν δὲ μὴ] οὗτοι ὦσι, μέχρ᾽ ἀνεψιότητος καὶ [ἀνεψιοῦ, ἐὰν ἅπαντες αἰδέσ]ασθαι ἐθέλωσι, τὸν κωλύοντα κρα[τεῖν] —"And if these do not exist, pardon is to be granted by those as far as the degree of cousin's son and cousin, if all are willing to grant it; the one who opposes it shall prevail" (Stroud's trans.). In view of the abundance of connectives everywhere else in the law, it is possible that a δέ or ἤ was inadvertently omitted by the scribe; or perhaps we should supplement line 15 differently, by writing ἐὰν μὴ πάντες instead of ἐὰν ἅπαντες. The variation between πάντες (line 15) and ἅπαντες (line 14) could be explained by the fact that the former is preceded by a vowel and the latter by a consonant, though the practice of Athenian inscriptions seems to be inconsistent in this regard. With this change we would translate the clause "unless all are willing to agree to a pardon, the one who opposes is to prevail."

tional by the Ephetai, for it is clear that the judging must
occur before the admission. Finally, since it is likely that
only relatives of a homicide victim could prosecute,[55] the
ten phratry members could be summoned only after a
conviction had been obtained by a relative who had later
died.

In the first two cases the timing of the pardon is not
made explicit, and it is possible that a reconciliation could
be reached before or even during a trial. But the order of
the provisions in the law suggests that trial and punishment
normally came first and pardon later, and two passages
in which Demosthenes discusses pardon (23.72, 37.58 =
38.22) show that this was the standard order of events
in the fourth century. I therefore think it likely that this
was also the normal procedure in Drakon's time.

The fact that only in this third case is it stated that the
killing must have been unintentional in order for the killer
to be pardoned seems to imply that this requirement does
not hold in the first two cases, and that the first two provisions thus apply to intentional as well as unintentional
homicide.[56] To avoid this implication one must either dif-
ferentiate in some way between ἄκων and μὴ ἐκ προνοίας
or agree that ἄκων needlessly introduces a restriction
already present by implication in the first two provisions
on pardon. We have already rejected (above, pp. 31–37)
the theory that killing ἄκων ("unintentionally") might be
a narrower category than killing μὴ ἐκ προνοίας ("not
intentionally"). On the other hand, if the mention of
ἄκων (line 17) is superfluous, why is there such emphasis
on the facts that the killing must have been ἄκων and
that the Ephetai must have decided that it was ἄκων? It is

55. See Gagarin, "The Prosecution of Homicide in Athens,"
GRBS 20 (1979):301–23.
56. See, e.g., Ruschenbusch, *"phonos,"* p. 138.

true that certification by the court of the unintentional nature of the homicide might be necessary in order to prevent an intentional killer who had fled without a trial from obtaining a pardon after claiming he had killed unintentionally. However, if pardon was in all cases restricted to unintentional killers, certification by the court would be just as necessary in the first two cases (where the relatives survive) as in the third, and we would expect the emphasis on the unintentional nature of the killing to come at the beginning of all the provisions for pardon. The mention of ἄκων only at the beginning of the third provision must indicate some difference between it and the first two provisions,[57] and we thus have no choice but to accept the prima facie implication of these lines, that the first two provisions are not limited to unintentional homicide.

It is unclear why pardon is emphatically restricted to those convicted of unintentional homicide only in the absence of living relatives. The large number of relatives included in the first two groups seems designed to render such situations rare, and it is likely that only under unusual circumstances would none of the victim's relatives survive. It is possible that Drakon was trying to discourage a killer and his relatives from trying to eliminate the surviving members of a homicide victim's family in order to obtain pardon from the ten phratry members, but this is merely a guess.

The third provision for pardon may have had a significant effect on the development of the idea of pardon. It

---

57. It is possible that the difference between the first two provisions and the third lay in some procedural detail, such as the necessity that a trial precede the pardon in the third case but not in the first two, but the emphatic double condition stipulating both unintentional homicide and a verdict by the Ephetai to that effect, seems to preclude this.

is generally accepted[58] that αἴδεσις originally referred to a monetary settlement between families,[59] of which we see traces in the epics.

If this was the case, then the first two clauses in the provisions for pardon would simply authorize and regulate this system, it being perhaps implied that the killer must go into exile before the pardon could be arranged by his family or friends. In the third case, however, when no relatives survived, admission to the city would constitute a true pardon, not something negotiated for money, since it seems unlikely that the phratry members could have accepted money from the killer. If this is the case, then Drakon is instituting a true, nonpurchased pardon, which is permitted, however, only in cases of unintentional homicide.

LINES 19–20

The provisions for pardon are followed immediately by a statement of retroactivity: καὶ οἱ δὲ πρότερον κτείναντες ἐν τῷδε τῷ θεσμῷ ἐνεχέσθων—"and let also those who killed previously be bound by this law." We cannot be certain exactly how many of the preceding provisions are meant to be included in this clause. The word θεσμός, like our word law, apparently could designate either a single provision or a group of provisions.[60] There are three indications, however, that θεσμός in the statement of retro-

---

58. See, e.g., Ruschenbusch, "phonos," p. 137.

59. Cf. the Patmos schol. ad Dem. 23.71 (BCH 1 [1877]:138): αἴδεσις δ' ἔστι τὸ δυσωπῆσαι ἱκετείᾳ καὶ χρήμασι τοὺς οἰκείους τοῦ πεφονευμένου.

60. In Solon's amnesty decree (Plut. Sol. 19) θεσμός apparently designates only the decree itself, whereas in the provision quoted in Dem. 23.62 it seems to designate all the homicide laws that have preceded.

activity designates the provisions concerning pardon but
no more.

First, the law in Dem. 43.57, from which this provision
is restored, contains the statement of retroactivity immediately following the first and third provisions for pardon,
even though retroactivity has no bearing on Demosthenes'
subject, the duties of relatives. This suggests that who-
ever inserted these laws in Demosthenes' text felt that the
statement of retroactivity belonged with the provisions
for pardon.

The second indication is a stylistic consideration. Most
new provisions after the opening of the law begin with an infinitive designating the main topic of the provision, followed
by δέ: δικάζειν δέ (lines 11–12), αἰδέσασθαι δέ (13), προειπεῖν δέ (20), συνδιώκειν δέ (21–22).[61] The effect of this
stylistic feature is to make the organization of the law
clearer, and it confirms the tacit assumption made earlier
that all the provisions for pardon in lines 13–19 form a
unit. It also suggests that the statement of retroactivity
which follows is part of this unit and applies only to these
provisions, since otherwise the statement of retroactivity
might have been written as a separate provision (e.g., ἐνέχεσθαι δέ . . .). Moreover, the connecting particles καί . . .
δέ[62] suggest a rather close connection with what preceded,[63]
and as we shall see (below, pp. 155–56), the arrangement

---

61. The one remaining complete provision (lines 26–29) does
not begin in the same manner, but the following provision (beginning
in line 30) probably did; see below.

62. See Stroud, p. 51, where he defends the addition of δέ (which
is not found in Dem. 43.57) to satisfy the stoichedon requirement of
line 20.

63. See Denniston, GP, p. 201: "Usually καί . . . δέ is taken in the
writer's stride . . . and follows a weak stop. Occasionally, however, it
marks a completely new start."

of the verbs and their subjects in lines 18–20 further links the two sentences.

The third indication is the content of the preceding provisions. It is evident that a provision for retroactivity would normally imply some innovation in the law, [64] and it is likely that the provisions for pardon were new, not only in providing for pardon by the phratry members when no relatives survived, but also in specifying precisely which relatives may grant pardon. If there was confusion about this matter in the period before Drakon's law (see above, pp. 15–16), then the provisions for pardon would have constituted a significant innovation and their retroactivity would be important.

It is possible, of course, that the first two provisions of the law (lines 11–13) also contained some innovations, but even if these provisions were new in some of their details there would be less need to make them retroactive, since most earlier homicides would already have been settled. On the other hand, retroactivity would be more important in the case of pardon, since the pardoning might occur many years after the original crime, and it would be undesirable to have two different systems for pardon existing simultaneously for perhaps two generations. The same consideration does not apply to the trial and punishment of the killer.

All these considerations make it likely that the provision for retroactivity was intended to apply exclusively to the provisions for pardon.

LINES 20–26

The statement of retroactivity seems to mark the end of the first section of the law, which contains the basic provisions for the treatment of homicide: the penalty, the

---

64. See Stroud, p. 51.

trial, and the possibility of pardon. The next section of
the law (lines 20–ca. 31) includes further procedural details
concerning the prosecution of a homicide and provisions
for the protection of the killer as long as he observes certain restrictions.

The section begins (lines 20–23) with two provisions
concerning prosecution: "A proclamation is to be made
against the killer (τῷ κτείναντι) in the agora by the victim's
relatives as far as the degree of cousin's son and cousin.
The prosecution is to be shared by the cousins and cousins'
sons and by sons-in-law, fathers-in-law, and phratry members." This implies that the duty to prosecute lay with the
agnate relatives, but the other relatives and phratry members were to assist them.

These provisions are among several laws concerning the
duties of relatives quoted in Dem. 43.57–58. No context
is specified, and had we only the quotation in Demosthenes,
we would no doubt assume that τῷ κτείναντι designated
the killer in general without regard to intent. It is conceiv-
able, however, that on our stele the provisions for proclamation and prosecution are meant to be understood solely
in the context of the law on unintentional homicide in
line 11.[65] In this case, the law in Dem. 43.57 may be copied
from this law on unintentional homicide or from a separate
law on intentional homicide containing identical provisions.[66]

---

65. This is Stroud's view (see, e.g., p. 52). He assumes that the
intervening provisions on the trial (and the planner of a homicide)
and on pardon have not altered the basic context of unintentional
homicide. See also MacDowell (pp. 118–20), who considers everything on the preserved inscription up to line 32 to apply to unintentional homicide only.

66. Note that the regulations for proclamation and prosecution
in Dem. 43.57 are followed by the first and third of the regulations
for pardon found in Drakon's law. Either Demosthenes has changed

That similar provisions for proclamation and prosecution were in force for cases of intentional homicide is
implied by the story of the killing of a noncitizen freedwoman, related in Dem. 47.52–73. From the speaker's
narration it is clear that the woman was the victim of an
intentional homicide,[67] and the law in this case required
relatives up to the degree of sons of cousins to prosecute
(κελεύει ὁ νόμος τοὺς προσήκοντας ἐπεξιέναι μέχρι ἀνε-
ψιαδῶν, 47.72). The speaker claims that he himself could
not prosecute since he was neither related to the woman
nor her master (she had once been his father's slave and
now was a free dependent of his living in his house).

Disregarding the many disputes concerning this passage,[68] I shall say simply that I believe it was normally
the duty of only the relatives of a citizen (or a master of a
slave[69]) to prosecute.[70] We do not know what the rule
was for freedmen, metics, or foreigners, many of whom
might have no relatives in Athens; it is quite possible
that the law did not provide specifically for these cases.
Indeed, the narrator's need to consult with the exegetai
and their inability to give him a clear statement of the
legal requirement in this case (most of their response is

---

the order of these provisions, or he is citing them from a different
source (see above, pp. 26–28) in which the order was different.

67. See above, pp. 33–34. The killer certainly intended to harm
the old woman, if not kill her (see Dem. 47.58–59).

68. I treat the problems of this passage among others at length
in "The Prosecution of Homicide in Athens," *GRBS* 20 (1979):301–
23.

69. Ant. 5.48: ἔξεστι . . . τῷ δεσπότῃ, ἂν δοκῇ, ἐπεξελθεῖν ὑπὲρ
τοῦ δούλου.

70. The procedure of *apagoge* was probably available to others
than the relatives of a homicide victim, but I do not believe any
others could bring a δίκη φόνου, nor do I believe in the existence of
a γραφὴ φόνου (see above, n. 68).

"advice") imply that this particular case was not covered explicitly by "the laws of Drakon on the stele" (τοὺς νόμους . . . τοὺς τοῦ Δράκοντος ἐκ τῆς στήλης, 47.71),[71] which the narrator himself consults. It is probable that the exegetai and the narrator consulted the provisions of Drakon's law relating to the intentional killing of a citizen[72] and perhaps also the killing of a slave and found that neither provision applied in this case. The law apparently did not preclude prosecution but made it inadvisable under the circumstances.

We may conclude, then, that although the case, had it been brought, would have been prosecuted at the Palladion (47.70) because of the woman's noncitizen status,[73] the law on prosecution mentioned in 47.72 concerns the prosecution of intentional homicide and indicates that the provisions for prosecution in this case were similar or identical to the provisions preserved on our stele (lines 20–23)[74] and in Dem. 43.57.[75] It is thus quite likely that the regulations concerning prosecution found on our stele were valid for both intentional and unintentional homicide, even if they may here be restricted by their context to unintentional homicide.

---

71. It is tempting to suppose that this stele is the very one that has survived; see Stroud, p. 40.

72. Cf. Stroud, pp. 39–40.

73. See *Ath. Pol.* 57.3.

74. Stroud (p. 52) is thus justified in using Dem. 47.72 to support his restoration μέχρι in line 21.

75. Pollux (8.118) in his discussion of the Areopagos states that prosecution for homicide (φόνου = intentional homicide; see below, p. 106) is allowed up to cousins (μέχρις ἀνεψιῶν). If his testimony is derived from Dem. 47, as Adolf Philippi (*Der Areopag und die Epheten* [Berlin, 1874], pp. 79–84) argued, then it supports the view that the laws discussed in Dem. 47 are those concerning intentional homicide.

These regulations are followed by a gap (lines 23–26) containing perhaps two more provisions. Though these cannot be restored, I suggest that the first (lines 23–25) may have concerned the protection afforded the accused killer before his trial,[76] and the second (25–26) the treatment of the convicted killer (φόνου ἕλωσ[ι]), perhaps providing for his safe passage into exile.[77] If these suggestions are in essence correct, the provisions would provide an orderly progression to lines 26–29; after provisions for the prosecution of a homicide we would have provisions setting forth the treatment of the killer before his trial, after his trial, and then in exile.

LINES 26–29

The next provision provides protection to the exiled killer: ἐὰν δέ τις τὸν ἀνδροφόνον κτείνῃ ἢ αἴτιος ᾖ φόνου ἀπεχόμενον ἀγορᾶς ἐφορίας καὶ ἄθλων καὶ ἱερῶν Ἀμφικτυονικῶν, ὥσπερ τὸν Ἀθηναῖον κτείναντα ἐν τοῖς αὐτοῖς ἐνέχεσθαι· διαγιγνώσκειν δὲ τοὺς ἐφέτας[78]—"If anyone kills the killer

---

76. αἴτιος [ᾖ] φό[νου] in 23–24 may form part of an expression similar to that in line 27; see Stroud, pp. 52–53.

77. Cf. Stroud, p. 53. Demosthenes tells us (23.72) that the law provided a safe passage into exile for the convicted unintentional killer.

78. As usually restored, lines 28 and 29 both violate the stoichedon requirement of 50 letters which is elsewhere strictly observed, as far as we can tell. The first has two extra letters, the second has one (see Stroud, p. 54). It seems unlikely that both anomalies are the result of scribal error. More probably either the law was slightly altered when inscribed on the stele from the Areopagus, or Demosthenes has altered it in his quotation (23.38). It is difficult to shorten line 28; one might try a shorter substitute for Ἀμφικτυονικῶν (Ἀμφικτυόνων?) or change the second καί to ἤ, but neither seems quite satisfactory. In line 29 Michael Jameson has suggested to me

or is responsible for his death, as long as he stays away from the frontier markets, games, and Amphiktyonic sacrifices, he shall be liable to the same treatment[79] as the one who kills an Athenian; and the Ephetai are to judge the case." That the provision refers to an exiled killer is implied by the stipulation that he must avoid frontier markets and the like for the law to be valid. The implication is also clear that if he is present in these places he will not be protected and may be killed with impunity.

Two points concerning the protected killer should be noted. First, it is likely that ἀνδροφόνος was the legal term for a convicted killer, as Demosthenes claims (23.29). Even though the orators sometimes use the term more loosely,[80] Drakon is careful to refer to the killer as τῷ κτείναντι before his trial (lines 20–21), but designates the convicted killer τὸν ἀνδροφόνον here and perhaps in line 30 (see below).[81] Thus, this provision designates protection specifically for the convicted killer, though in effect it probably included all killers.[82]

Second, the term ἀνδροφόνος in itself gives no indication

---

that the Drakontian form for the masculine dative plural may have been –οισι (see K. Meisterhans, *Grammatik der attischen Inschriften*, 3d ed., [Berlin, 1900], p. 126, n. 1129); if we write ἐν τοῖσι αὐτοῖσι and then make the simple change of διαγιγνώσκειν to διαγνῶναι (cf. line 13), we have the required fifty letters.

79. For the sense of ἐν τοῖς αὐτοῖς ἐνέχεσθαι see above, n. 30.

80. For references see Stroud, p. 53; he rejects Demosthenes' claim.

81. The phrase οἱ πρότερον κτείναντες in lines 19–20 may designate only convicted killers, but here the participle is necessary because of the temporal qualification πρότερον.

82. If a killer immediately went into exile without contesting the case in a trial, it is likely that after a proclamation by the victim's relatives the basileus would formally adjudge the killer guilty, and he would then legally be an ἀνδροφόνος.

whether the protection applies to an intentional or unintentional killer or to both. Demosthenes, however, quotes
the law among the laws of the Areopagos (23.37), and
his discussion of this provision (23.37–43) does not suggest any restriction to intentional or unintentional homicide. It seems likely, then, that this provision applies to
all exiled killers, regardless of intent.[83]

The law grants protection to the exiled killer by declaring that one who kills him or is responsible for his death
"shall be liable to the same treatment as the one who kills
an Athenian." Again no intent is specified;[84] presumably the intentional killing of an exiled killer was treated
like the intentional killing of an Athenian and an unintentional killing like the unintentional killing of an Athenian. The primary purpose of the clause, however, must
have been to prevent the intentional killing of the exiled
killer. In early times killers could be pursued in exile
and the risk of such pursuit may well have persisted till
Drakon's time. Indeed, the hypothetical case suggested
by Demosthenes (23.42–43), which would fall under this
provision of the homicide law if it were not for Aristo-
krates' special decree, is precisely such a case of a homicide victim's friends seizing and killing the exiled killer.
The law in lines 26–29, then, applies to any killing of the

---

83. Cf. the law in Dem. 23.44, where the property of exiled
killers whose property has not been confiscated (τῶν ἀνδροφόνων
τῶν ἐξεληλυθότων ὧν τὰ χρήματα ἐπίτιμα) is protected against
seizure. It is the qualifying phrase, as Demosthenes points out, which
restricts the application of ἀνδροφόνων in this case to unintentional
killers.

84. The expression αἴτιος φόνου in line 27 presumably designates
the planner of a homicide as distinct from the actual killer, and may
thus in itself imply intentional homicide. Also, φόνος without qualification suggests intentional homicide (see below, p. 106).

exiled killer, regardless of intent, but envisions primarily the case of intentional killing in revenge.

LINES 30-36

The provision that follows cannot be reconstructed with certainty, but it probably allowed a killer caught in Attica to be killed or arrested. On the basis of the law in Dem. 23.28 Stroud (p. 55, n. 102) suggests restoring lines 30-31 as follows: [ἐξ]εῖ[ναι δὲ τοὺς ἀνδροφόνους ἀποκτείνειν ἢ ἀπάγειν, ἐὰν ἐν] τῇ ἡμεδ[απῇ]. . . .—"It is allowed to kill or to arrest killers if [they are caught] in the territory."[85]

As in the preceding clause, the term ἀνδροφόνος probably indicates that the provision applied only to convicted killers, and it is also likely that the provision applied to both the intentional and the unintentional killer who did not go into (or who returned from) exile. The law in Dem. 23.28, which refers to and expands upon this clause, applies to intentional killers, as Demosthenes' discussion makes clear (23.29-36), but it is likely that the convicted unintentional killer had similar protection.

The next two lines (33-35)[86] are not fully restorable, but lines 33-34 appear to contain the phrase [ἄρχον]τα χειρῶν ἀ[δίκων], which was the legal term for beginning a fight.[87] If we accept the common restoration of lines 34-

---

85. The only difficulty with this restoration is that Drakon otherwise uses the simple verb κτείνω eight times but never the compound ἀποκτείνω. Nonetheless, Stroud's suggestion is likely to be in essence correct, even if it needs to be slightly reworded (e.g., καὶ κτείνειν κἀπάγειν).

86. It is possible that the provision beginning in line 30 ended in line 31 or 32 and that another matter was treated before the provision on killing in self-defense began in 33; if so, we have no idea what this might have been.

87. In the restoration only χειρῶν is reasonably certain. The

35, [χειρ]ῶν ἀδίκων κτεί[νῃ],[88] the provision concerning
the killing of someone who starts a fight would extend at
least as far as this line and probably as far as τοὺς ἐ[φέτ]ας
in lines 35–36.[89] In any case, it is likely that at least in
lines 33–34 a provision existed allowing a plea of self-
defense in a fight started by the homicide victim.

I have elsewhere discussed more fully the plea of self-
defense in homicide cases and have concluded that such
a plea probably did not bring the case into the category of
lawful homicide, which would be tried at the Delphinion
if a trial was necessary.[90] Rather, a plea of self-defense
would be entered in a trial for intentional homicide at the
Areopagos (in the fourth century, at least). The defendant
could probably be acquitted if he could show that the
victim did indeed start the fight and that his own retaliation was a reasonable and necessary defensive action. The
case, like all other homicide cases in Drakon's law, would
be tried by the Ephetai (see below, Chapter Seven).

LINES 36–38

The final provision that can be reconstructed in the inscription of Drakon's law is a true example of a case of lawful
homicide. The provision probably begins in line 36, since
the expression [διαγιγνώσκει]ν δὲ τοὺς ἐ[φέτ]ας seems to
mark the end of the preceding provision (cf. lines 13, 29),

---

other two words were originally suggested by Köhler and have been
accepted by most editors since. Stroud's three new letters all fit
this restoration. For ἄρχων χειρῶν ἀδίκων see Gagarin, "Self-
defense," p. 115, n. 19.

88. The restoration of 34–35 is uncertain, since the only complete word may be interpreted as ἄδικον, in which case the possibilities for restoring what precedes are almost unlimited.

89. See Stroud, p. 56.

90. Gagarin, "Self-defense."

and there does not seem to be room in line 36 for another complete provision. If the letters EI near the beginning of line 37 represent the subjunctive ᾖ, then a conditional clause probably preceded, which would likely have concerned the status of the lawful killer: [ἐὰν δέ τις . . .] ΕΙΣ ἢ ἐλεύθερος ᾖ, κα[ὶ ἐάν . . .].[91]

The main restorable portion of the law reads: καὶ ἐὰν φέροντα ἢ ἄγοντα βίᾳ ἀδίκως εὐθὺς ἀμυνόμενος κτείνῃ, νηποινεὶ τεθνάναι—"And if he defending himself straightaway kills someone forcibly and unjustly[92] plundering or seizing him, the victim shall die without [the killer paying] a penalty."[93] The law is reconstructed from its quotation in Dem. 23.60, and Demosthenes' discussion of it (23.60–61) clarifies its meaning to some extent. Apparently it concerns the attempt forcibly to seize either a person (with the intent of ransoming him) or his property,[94] and it seems to suggest the activity of pirates or highwaymen rather than burglars (who could also be killed if caught in one's home at night; Dem. 24.113). Anyone who killed someone making such an attempt would pay no penalty.

Apparently there was no express provision for a trial, since there is not room in line 38 for the shortest

---

91. This clause would provide a τις, which is lacking in the restored portion (lines 37–38). Borimir Jordon notes that ἐλεύθερος occurs only in very early Athenian inscriptions or in copies of early inscriptions (*Servants of the Gods* [*Hypomnemata*, vol. 55, Göttingen, 1979]), p. 39.

92. The qualification ἀδίκως may be intended to exclude cases of lawful seizure of property, such as property owed after a court settlement, which sometimes had to be seized by force.

93. Originally, and perhaps still in Drakon's time, νηποινεὶ meant "without recompense," though by the fifth century at least, when the system of paying blood money (ποινή) to the victim's family was obsolete, it must have been understood to mean "without penalty."

94. See Gagarin, "Self-defense," p. 113, n. 9

declaration to that effect (διαγνῶναι δὲ τοὺς ἐφέτας) unless the next sentence begins with an anomalous asyndeton. Moreover, in none of the other laws describing circumstances in which homicide is lawful is there any explicit provision for a trial.[95] Probably a general provision, which either came later in the law or was enacted after Drakon's time, allowed disputed cases of lawful homicide to be decided at the Delphinion.

These are all the provisions whose restoration on the inscription is reasonably certain. When considered as a whole they form, I think, a clear, well ordered sequence of regulations. The penalty is naturally stated first. It is followed by the designation of a trial by the basileis and the Ephetai, together with the important principle that a planner of a homicide is also included in the law. Then come retroactive provisions for pardoning the convicted killer. The next portion of the law gives details regarding the proclamation against the killer, the prosecution, the protection of the killer before trial (?), the carrying out of the sentence (?), the protection of the exiled killer, and the penalty for a killer who returns unlawfully. The restorable text ends with a provision for self-defense and one case of lawful homicide.

The one puzzling feature of this arrangement is that the law apparently begins with a provision for unintentional homicide without mentioning the crime of intentional homicide, which must have been both more common and of greater concern to Drakon than unintentional homicide. It is to this peculiarity that we must now address ourselves.

---

95. Ibid., pp. 119–20.

CHAPTER FOUR

THE LAW ON INTENTIONAL HOMICIDE

The question, why does our inscription not begin with the law on intentional homicide, immediately raises two further, related questions: where was the Athenian law on intentional homicide to be found after the reinscription of Drakon's homicide law in 409/8? and where was the law on intentional homicide when Drakon first wrote his homicide law? It is easiest to group the many answers to these questions into three possible answers to the last question, which we shall examine in turn: Drakon wrote no law on intentional homicide; Drakon wrote a law on intentional homicide and placed it at the beginning of his homicide law on his first axon; or Drakon wrote a law on intentional homicide and placed it later in his law, after all the provisions preserved on our stele.

The possibility that Drakon wrote no law on intentional homicide is suggested by Busolt-Swoboda (p. 811). They observe that the opening sentence of the preserved law lacks the proper connecting particle δέ (we shall return to this point in Chapter Five) and conclude that it is therefore not a fragment of a longer law but a self-contained amendment (*Novelle*) to an already existing law that treated φόνος pure and simple. In their view Drakon, who was the first to distinguish among intentional, unintentional, and lawful homicide, left the existing law intact to cover the first category and added his new law concerning unintentional and lawful homicide as an amendment. Thus, the law on intentional homicide was never considered part of Drakon's law on homicide and was not republished as part of it in 409/8.

There are two serious objections to this theory. First, if Drakon was the first to divide homicide law into these three categories, it is difficult to explain how he could have made the traditional law concerning all homicide apply only to intentional homicide without either changing the wording of the traditional law or making some special reference to it at the beginning of his new law (e.g., "The traditional law will apply to cases of intentional homicide, and if. . . ."). In the first case he would in effect have written a law on intentional homicide, which should have been preserved as part of his law; in the second case his opening remark should have been preserved as part of his law.

Second, even if Drakon did not himself write the law on intentional homicide, it was always considered part of Drakon's homicide law by the Athenians.[1] The evidence for this is clear: Demosthenes twice explicitly names Drakon as the author of laws on intentional homicide (20.158, 23.51);[2] moreover, in another case (Dem. 47.71) the speaker consults "the laws of Drakon on the stele" in order to learn what to do about the intentional killing of a freedwoman in his house, and the law he consulted was almost certainly the law on intentional homicide (see above, pp. 56–57). Indeed, the expression "the laws of Drakon on the stele" seems to mean simply the official laws on homicide, including intentional homicide. Even if these speakers are mistaken in their attribution to Drakon of the law on intentional homicide, this view must have been in accordance with the general opinion of the Athenian public.

---

1. See Stroud, pp. 35–36.
2. On Dem. 20.158 see Stroud, p. 38.

In addition to this clear positive evidence there is the further consideration that not a shred of evidence exists to suggest that the Athenians considered anyone other than Drakon the author of the laws on intentional homicide. We have Aristotle's testimony [3] that Solon did not alter Drakon's homicide laws; Peisistratos did not change the offices or laws he found in existence (Herod. 1.59.6); and Ephialtes' reforms of the Areopagos, whatever they were, do not seem to have affected the substance of the homicide laws. [4] In short, no name other than Drakon's is ever attached to the Athenian homicide laws.

Even if this view was wrong, and if some Athenian officials knew that in fact the law on intentional homicide was not Drakon's, a decree of the assembly could not have used the expression τὸν Δράκοντος νόμον τὸν περὶ τοῦ φόνου to designate all homicide laws except the law on intentional homicide unless this implication was generally recognized, and clearly it was not. Furthermore, as we shall see later (p. 106), φόνος alone often implies intentional homicide and certainly could not be used without qualification to designate only unintentional and lawful homicide. Thus it seems necessary to conclude that when the decree was passed in 409/8 calling for the republication of "Drakon's law on homicide," the assembly must have intended to include the law on intentional homicide in the republication. [5]

In sum, it seems impossible that Drakon could have added provisions concerning only unintentional and lawful homicide to a traditional law concerning all homicide on the unexpressed assumption that the traditional law would

---

3. *Ath. Pol.* 7.1; cf. Plut. *Sol.* 17.

4. See Philochoros *FGH* 328 F64.

5. For the difficult question of whether amendments later than Drakon's time were inscribed on the stele see above, pp. 28–29.

thenceforth be the law on intentional homicide, and even if Drakon had done this, the law on intentional homicide was considered his in 409/8 and would have been inscribed on the stele as part of "Drakon's law on homicide."

We can now turn to the second possibility, that Drakon's law on intentional homicide preceded the law on unintentional homicide but for some reason was not republished with it in 409/8. There are a number of different reasons given for the absence of the law on the preserved stele, and these can conveniently be divided into two groups.

The first group of scholars assume that the original law on intentional homicide, which preceded the preserved law, still existed and was considered Drakon's in 409/8 but was not inscribed on the preserved stele. Three different explanations for its absence have been given: Köhler[6] thought there was no room on the preserved stele and thus suggested that the law on intentional homicide was reinscribed at the same time on a separate stele, which stood next to the preserved one; the text of the decree was presumably inscribed at the head of both stelai. Schreiner[7] suggested that the decree of 409/8 called for a revision of the existing homicide laws, that the law on intentional homicide needed no revision, and that the anagrapheis therefore left the law on intentional homicide in its original form, and on a stele next to it inscribed first the decree and then the law on unintentional homicide, which was in need of revision. Finally, Harrison[8] suggested that the words Πρῶτος ῎Αξων on the inscription (line 10) are not a heading for that section of the law but stand for "the

---

6. *Hermes* 2 (1867): 36.

7. J. Schreiner, *De corpore iuris Atheniensium* (Bonn, 1913), p. 90.

8. *CQ*, n.s. 11 (1961):3–5.

contents of the first axon," namely the law on intentional homicide. Thus, the anagrapheis left the first axon intact and on the new stele they inscribed "Drakon's law on homicide" as follows: "First Axon [*sc.* the law on intentional homicide] plus (καί) if a man not intentionally kills. . . ." The reason for this unusual procedure was that the first axon was still in good physical condition, whereas the law on unintentional homicide was deteriorating and needed to be reinscribed.

A number of objections to these views have been raised by Stroud (pp. 35–40). The major difficulties are as follows: first, the preserved decree states, "Let the scribes inscribe Drakon's law on homicide" (τὸν Δράκοντος νόμον τὸν περὶ τοῦ φόνου ἀναγραψάντων οἱ ἀναγραφεῖς). Stroud rightly emphasizes that the decree calls for re-publication, not for revision,[9] and argues forcefully[10] on the basis of certain obsolete features in the law (especially the provision for retroactivity and the mention of frontier markets) that the preserved inscription is a true copy (or virtually so) of Drakon's original law. Stroud also notes (pp. 54–56) that the amendment cited in Dem. 23.28, which probably refers to a provision on the stele (lines 30–31), was not inscribed here in place of the original provision, and that this further supports the hypothesis of verbatim re-publication rather than revision.

Furthermore, the wording of the decree seems to leave no doubt that the whole of Drakon's law on homicide is to be published, not merely some part of it, and that it is to be published on a single stele (line 7); the reference in Dem. 47.71 to "the laws of Drakon on the stele" (ἐκ τῆς στήλης) also implies the existence of only one stele

---

9. For ἀναγράφω meaning "publish" see the works cited by Stroud, p. 20.

10. See esp. pp. 60–64.

containing Drakon's laws. These considerations pose
serious difficulties for all three views. Finally, Stroud
recovered enough new letters to demonstrate convincingly (pp. 16–18) the existence of a second heading,
Δεύτερος Ἄξων, in line 56. This discovery invalidates
Harrison's ingenious theory and also eliminates Köhler's
only argument.

In view of these objections and others[11] we must
reject all these explanations, which assume that Drakon's
law on intentional homicide still existed in its original
form in 409/8 but was not republished on the stele that
survives.

The most prevalent opinion concerning the law on
intentional homicide is that it originally stood at the
beginning of Drakon's law before the law on unintentional
homicide, but that it was revised at some time before
409/8 and was thus no longer considered part of Drakon's
law on homicide when this law was republished.[12] According to this hypothesis the opening word καί originally connected the two laws, and after the revision and removal
of the first law on intentional homicide καί remained as
the opening word, though no longer serving any purpose.
The reason generally given for the revision of the law
was the desire to transfer jurisdiction in cases of intentional
homicide to the Areopagos; Drakon in this view had left
such cases either to self-help or to the Ephetai to judge (see
below, pp. 125–37).

This position is susceptible to the same basic objection
raised above, that the decree calls for the re-publication

_____

11. See Stroud, p. 35.

12. Among recent proponents of this view are Kurt Latte (*RE*
20.1 [1941]:526) and Ruschenbusch ("*phonos,*" pp. 130–31); see
Stroud, p. 35, n. 20 for further references.

of Drakon's law on homicide and that the Athenians of the fifth and fourth centuries considered Drakon alone to be the author of all their homicide laws, including the law on intentional homicide. Even if this opinion was not historically accurate, it is the only one expressed in any of our sources, and it is almost inconceivable that at the end of the fifth century the law on intentional homicide was not included among the provisions of "Drakon's law on homicide."

Another obstacle to this view is the presence of καί at the beginning of the law on the preserved stele. If καί originally connected the law on intentional homicide to the law on unintentional homicide, why was it not deleted when the first law was removed for revision? And if καί was originally left at the beginning of the unrevised law by mistake, would not the anagrapheis who republished the law have been aware that this was an error and have deleted the word? [13]

This objection is not as strong as the first, since it is possible, however unlikely, that καί somehow survived scrutiny and was reinscribed by mistake. Nonetheless, the major difficulty remains to explain what could have happened to the law on intentional homicide after it was revised, and why it was not republished in 409/8 if it was still considered part of Drakon's law on homicide, as it seems it must have been.

---

13. See Schreiner (above, n. 7), p. 77 and Stroud, p. 37. D. M. Lewis (*CR,* n.s. 21 [1971]:390–91) suggests that the anagrapheis' fidelity to the original wording in the text of the law may be an argument in favor of their having preserved καί at the beginning, but given that they would undoubtedly have been aware that the survival of καί at the beginning of the law was simply a mistake, the case is not really the same as, say, their preservation of an obsolete statement of retroactivity.

A further difficulty, which we shall consider at length in the next chapter, is the meaning and use of καί. I shall argue that καί probably would not have been used to connect the laws on intentional and unintentional homicide; rather, the connective would have been δέ.

We come now to the third possibility, that the provisions concerning intentional homicide came later in Drakon's law, after all the preserved provisions. A corollary of this view is that καί originally stood at the beginning of the law just as it does in the preserved inscription, and that it must therefore have the adverbial sense "even." This possibility was suggested by Stroud (pp. 37–40),[14] who may have been inspired by his discovery of the new heading Δεύτερος Ἄξων later in the inscription (line 56). This second heading indicates that the text of Drakon's law was longer than most scholars had previously thought and that there was certainly enough room on the stele for provisions concerning intentional homicide.

No one has disputed the reading [Δεύτ]ερος [Ἄξων],[15] but Stroud's theory that the law on intentional homicide came later in the law has met with a mixed reception and has been rejected by several reviewers, primarily because of the difficulty of beginning a law with καί ἐάν in the sense of "even if."[16] I shall consider the problem of καί ἐάν at length in the next two chapters; for the moment I wish to raise a number of other objections to Stroud's view.

---

14. Stroud was not the first to suggest that the initial καί means "even." Maschke (p. 46) assumes this meaning for καί, and Busolt-Swoboda (p. 811) allow that it may mean either "and" or "even."

15. See Stroud, pp. 16–18, 58–60; the large size of the letters makes the restoration virtually certain.

16. See B. M. Caven, *JHS* 91 (1971):193; Ruschenbusch, *Gnomon* 46 (1974):816; and D. M. Lewis, *CR,* n.s. 21 (1971):391; cf. Sealey, pp. 101–02.

The first difficulty is simply the inherent improbability
that Drakon left the provisions on intentional homicide
till the end of his law, where they would follow not only
the law on unintentional homicide but also the provisions
for pardon, prosecution, protection of the exiled killer,
self-defense, and lawful homicide, as well as several other
provisions no longer preserved. I acknowledge an element
of subjectivity in this judgment; there is no reason why
Drakon could not have arranged his law in any order he
wished, however arbitrary or unreasonable it might seem
to us. Nonetheless, I consider it very unlikely that Drakon left his law on intentional homicide until the end.

One reason for this conviction is that although other
Greek laws, such as those at Gortyn, may take up different
general topics in an apparently arbitrary order, within a
general topic regulations are usually presented in a clear
and reasonable order: from the more general to the more
specific, from the more to the less serious, from the more
to the less common, or from certain actions to others
arising out of those actions. In the first section of the Gortyn laws (I.2–II.2), for example, fines for unlawful seizure
of a free man always precede those for the unlawful seizure of a slave; in the second section (II.2–10) the various
categories of rape are generally ordered from the more
to the less serious;[17] and in a late fifth-century inscription
from Thasos (*GHI* 83) provisions concerning treason in
the city precede those concerning treason in the colonies.
The arrangement of these and other provisions in Greek

---

17. The order of offenses is (a) rape of a free person by a free
person and then by a slave, and (b) rape of a slave by a free person
and then by a slave. The fines are not in descending order—the
fine is double when the rapist is a slave—but the sequence of
offenses is clear and reasonable and probably did represent a decreasing order of seriousness.

laws may not be precisely the same as in modern law, but
it is clear and reasonable, and it reinforces an expectation
that the provisions of Drakon's homicide law will prove
to have been reasonably ordered.

This expectation is confirmed by the existing provisions,
which are clearly and reasonably arranged to deal with the
problem of homicide in Drakon's time. It therefore seems
inexplicable that the law on intentional homicide should
have been left to the end. Not only is it likely to have been
a more common and more serious offense than unintentional homicide, but the primary purpose of Drakon's law
(as with any comprehensive homicide law) must have
been to legislate for cases of intentional, not unintentional,
homicide. It is not impossible that Drakon may have had
some special reason for leaving the law on intentional homicide till the end of his law, but it is much more likely
that the law on intentional homicide stood at the beginning.
It is worth noting that if it did stand at the beginning, the
order—intentional, unintentional, lawful homicide—would
be the same as the order of the discussion of the Athenian
homicide courts in both Demosthenes (23.65–75) and
Aristotle (*Ath. Pol.* 57.3).[18]

In support of his hypothesis that intentional homicide
came later in Drakon's law, Stroud (p. 40) adduces the
section on homicide in Plato's *Laws* (865A–874B), which
"gives first place to unpremeditated homicide; murder
is discussed last." In fact, the discussion of homicide begins
at 864E3 (πλὴν ἂν ἄρα τινὰ ἀποκτείνας), where in the con-

---

18. Cantarella, p. 89, is troubled not only by the fact that in
Stroud's theory the first crime is the less serious one, but also by the fact
that it is negatively defined (ἐὰν μὴ ἐκ προνοίας . . .). It seems to
be a general rule (see, e.g., Gortyn V.9–17, VIII.30–36) that when
two successive legal provisions apply to conditions one of which
is the negative of the other, the positive condition is stated first.

text of crimes committed by madmen Plato takes up the case
of homicide by madmen. Beginning with this case[19] Plato
proceeds to discuss unintentional lawful homicide (865A3–
B4); unintentional homicide (865B4–866D4); homicide
in anger (866D5–869C6); homicide in self-defense (869C6–
E8); intentional homicide, including suicide (869E10–
873D8); killing by animals, inanimate objects, and unknown
killers (873E1–874B5); and finally, intentional lawful
homicide (874B6–D1).[20]

Plato's discussion does proceed roughly in the direction
of the increasing responsibility of the killer, and unintentional does precede intentional killing, but the correspondence with Stroud's hypothetical arrangement of Drakon's
law is not close enough to suggest any connection. Moreover, many other passages in the *Laws* show an arrangement
inconsistent with the general rules of actual Greek laws as
outlined above. The law on temple robbery, for example,
treats slaves and foreigners first (854D1–E1) and citizens
second (854E1–855A4). The laws on assault begin with the
case of a foreigner assaulting a citizen (879D5–E6). This
may be the result of the unrevised nature of the work, or
of design: Saunders notes a habit of Plato's "to let one
topic launch him into a discussion of another,"[21] and this
is precisely the case with the homicide laws, which arise
rather suddenly from the context of crimes committed by
madmen. In view of this, the parallels between Plato's
discussion of homicide and the hypothetical arrangement
of Drakon's law provide little support for Stroud's view.

In addition to the inherent improbability that Drakon

---

19. φόνου δὴ καθάπερ ἠρξάμεθα, 865A1.

20. Stroud's reference (p. 40, n. 34) to the *Laws* gives 874B as
the end of the section on homicide; this is apparently a misprint
for 874D.

21. Plato, *The Laws*, trans. T. J. Saunders (London, 1970), p. 38.

began his law with a law on unintentional homicide, other difficulties with this hypothesis arise from the remaining provisions of the law. As we saw in Chapter Three, the provision making the planner equally responsible for a homicide implies a context of intentional homicide, and the provisions on pardon in two of the three cases apply by implication to both intentional and unintentional homicide. It is difficult to see how these provisions could be preceded by nothing but a law on unintentional homicide, as Stroud supposes.

The provisions that come after the section on pardon and before the provision for self-defense are all unrestricted with respect to intent; the offender is designated simply "the killer": οἱ κτείναντες (lines 19–20), τῷ κτείναντι (20–21), τὸν ἀνδροφόνον (27–28 and perhaps 30).[22] Moreover, as far as we can tell, in all these cases the provisions for intentional and unintentional homicide were the same.

If the law on intentional homicide originally stood at the head of Drakon's law together with the law on unintentional homicide, all these provisions are naturally and easily understood to apply to both intentional and unintentional homicide. If, on the other hand, the law on intentional homicide came later and these provisions are meant to apply only to unintentional homicide, then either they would all have to be repeated in the section on intentional homicide or there would have to be a series of cross-references in that section back to these provisions.[23]

---

22. For the law in line 30 see above, chap. 3. If the amendment referring to this law (Dem. 23.28) concerns intentional homicide, as it apparently must, and if the emendation ἐν τῷ ⟨α⟩ ἄξονι is correct (see above, chap. 2, n. 44), then the law in line 30 must refer to intentional as well as unintentional homicide.
23. See Stroud, p. 40, n. 33.

Though not impossible, neither alternative is attractive. Repetition of brief, almost formulaic phrases (e.g., διαγι-γνώσκεν δὲ τοὺς ἐφέτας) is common in Greek law, indeed in all law, but the repetition of entire provisions occurs rarely, and it is hard to imagine a repetition of a dozen or more lines later in the law.[24] Cross-references are also rare in Greek law,[25] and although a series of them would probably not be as awkward as a series of repetitions, one would expect the full provisions to be given in the law on intentional homicide with cross-references in the law on unintentional homicide rather than vice versa. In any case the question remains, why would Drakon have arranged his law in such a way as to require such repetition or cross-reference, when the simpler arrangement would be to begin with the law on intentional homicide (followed immediately by the law on unintentional homicide)?

The provision granting protection to the exiled killer (lines 26–29) raises a special difficulty for Stroud's theory. Here the rule is that anyone who kills an exiled killer or is responsible for his death is to be liable to the same treatment as the one who kills an Athenian. Although there is no explicit mention of intent in the provision,[26] it is obvious that the primary purpose of such a provision must be to protect the exiled killer against being killed intentionally,

---

24. In the Hekatompedon inscription (*IG* I^2.4 [I^3.4]) a provision is repeated in identical words (lines 6–8, 11–13), but it is likely that these provisions were originally enacted separately and then reinscribed together on this inscription (see below, chap. 8, n. 6).

25. Cf. Drakon's law, lines 28–29. At Gortyn cross-references are used (e.g., VIII.29–30) in the complicated sections on inheritance; they refer to nearby provisions and there appears to be no simpler way of avoiding them. In an amendment, of course, cross-reference to an existing law is to be expected (e.g., Dem. 23.28).

26. But see above, chap. 3, n. 84.

most likely by friends or relatives of the victim seeking
revenge. The statement that such a homicide is to be
treated like the killing of an Athenian implies that the
law concerning the intentional killing of an Athenian
has already been stated. It is not impossible that the reader
of the law had to look further in the inscription to find
the provision for intentional homicide, but the alternative,
that the law on intentional homicide originally preceded
this clause, seems much more probable.

Finally, the provisions for self-defense (lines 33–36)
and for lawful homicide (37–38) suggest that the law on
intentional homicide has already been stated. If, as I
have maintained, a plea of self-defense was entered at a
trial for intentional homicide, the presence of this provision would seem to require an earlier statement of the
law on intentional homicide. And the provision allowing the killing of someone plundering one's property or
seizing one's person also envisions the possibility that
a charge of intentional homicide would otherwise be
brought in such a case. Here too one would expect that
the law on intentional homicide had already been stated.

All these considerations point to the same conclusion, that the law on intentional homicide originally stood
at or near the beginning of Drakon's homicide law. It may
be that no single consideration in itself proves that the law
on intentional homicide could not have come later in the
law, but each raises serious difficulties for Stroud's hypothesis, and their cumulative weight is overwhelming.

One further difficulty noted by several reviewers[27] is
the implication that if Drakon began his law with καὶ ἐάν
in the sense of "even if," the law on intentional homicide ought to have already been stated. Stroud provides
little explanation as to why Drakon might have wished

27. See above, n. 16.

thus to emphasize his opening statement or what the implication of that emphasis might be. I shall discuss this objection in the course of examining the implication of καὶ ἐάν in the next two chapters.

We are now left with the following conclusions: first, Drakon must have written a law on intentional homicide or else incorporated an existing law into his homicide law, and this law ought to have been re-published in 409/8 on the stele containing "Drakon's law on homicide." Second, if the law on intentional homicide originally preceded the law on unintentional homicide, there is no adequate explanation for its absence from our stele. Third, there are a number of serious objections to the hypothesis that the law on intentional homicide stood later in the law, on the portion of the stele no longer preserved.

Together these conclusions lead to one question: if the law on intentional homicide originally stood neither before nor after the law on unintentional homicide, where was it? As we shall see, there is a solution, and it requires a close examination of the use of καὶ εἰ in Greek legal texts.

καὶ εἰ IN GREEK LAWS

The most common theory concerning the law on intentional homicide is that it originally preceded the law on unintentional homicide and that καί (= "and"), which is the first word in the preserved law, originally connected the two laws. As we saw, there are serious difficulties with this view and Stroud rejected it, proposing instead that καί originally began the law in the adverbial sense of "even."

Stroud based his interpretation of καί primarily on arguments that the law on intentional homicide did not originally come first in the inscription. If we leave aside for the moment the question of intentional homicide in Drakon's law and examine simply the use of καὶ εἰ in Greek legal texts, we must conclude that καί in its sense "and" would probably not have been used to connect the law on intentional homicide to the law on unintentional homicide, and thus is probably used adverbially (= "even") at the beginning of Drakon's law. This chapter presents the evidence from other Greek laws; the next considers the implications of καὶ ἐάν in Drakon's law.

To my knowledge only Busolt-Swoboda (p. 811) have objected on the ground of usage to the view that καί originally connected two provisions of Drakon's law, maintaining that the correct connective in such a case would be δέ. They rightly compare the Gortyn laws and note (p. 812) that in these "sind die fortlaufenden Einzelbestimmungen regelmässig mit αἰ δέ κα miteinander verbunden."

They conclude that whether καί means "and" or "even," it must originally have been the first word in Drakon's law and not a connective joining the preserved text to a preceding law. Busolt-Swoboda's conclusion has generally been ignored, perhaps because their overall theory about Drakon's law (see above, Chapter Four) is unconvincing. Their conclusion about the use of καί and δέ, however, is valid, as I hope to demonstrate by examining sentences in Greek laws beginning with a conditional clause.[1]

That δέ is the most common particle introducing a legal provision in the form of a conditional sentence is clear from a quick perusal of any body of Greek laws, such as the laws at Gortyn,[2] those found scattered through the Attic orators, or collections of inscriptions. καὶ εἰ[3] does occur occasionally, however, and we must look closely at these cases in order to determine as precisely as possible the reasons for and limitations on its use. We shall not find firm rules covering all cases, but rather general guidelines for most cases. There are a few specific cases in which the use of καί as a connective seems to be prohibited.

It will be helpful, first, to distinguish within the general class of legal provisions two forms of legal statement, legal regulations and legal sanctions.

I shall define a legal regulation as the statement of a legally prescribed procedure to be followed in a specific case. A regulation may be in the form of a condition (e.g., "If there are no living relatives, the Ephetai are to appoint

---

1. Conditional sentences are common in Greek laws, as indeed in most laws; see Stroud, p. 40.

2. A quick count in the Gortyn laws reveals eighty-six instances of αἰ δέ beginning a legal provision compared with seven occurrences of καί (= καὶ αἰ), only three of which begin new provisions.

3. I shall use the form καὶ εἰ to represent all dialectical forms and also contractions with ἄν.

ten phratry members.") or a simple statement (e.g., "The Ephetai are to decide the case.").

In contrast, a legal sanction is the statement of a legally prescribed penalty for a specific act of wrongdoing. In Greek laws a sanction is virtually always expressed as a third-person conditional sentence; the offense is stated in the protasis and the penalty in the apodosis (e.g., "If a man kills another, he is exiled."). Legal sanctions in this form are the regular means for expressing legislation in most societies, and it has been said that there is no true law without them.[4]

There is not always a clear demarcation between these two kinds of statement, since the procedure expressed in some regulations may be seen from another point of view as a sanction. At Gortyn (II.52–54), for example, in a divorce case the woman shall have "an additional five staters if the husband is the cause of the divorce." This provision is stated as part of the regulations concerning the property that belongs to the wife in a divorce case and I would consider it a regulation. It might be said, however, that the five staters represent a fine and the act of causing the divorce the offense, and that the statement is in fact a legal sanction; but as it stands in the law, the provision is presented as a regulation.[5] Despite possibly ambiguous cases like this, most examples are quite clear and this division into regulations and sanctions will serve our purpose.

There are four possible sequential combinations of regulations and sanctions, each of which can be further divided into two possibilities as follows:

---

4. See Diamond, p. 45.

5. In some cases the precise wording of a provision will be important in determining whether it is presented as a regulation or a sanction; see below pp. 90–91.

a. A regulation may be followed by another regulation
that either (i) adds something further to the first
regulation or (ii) states the procedure to be followed
in a different case. It is sometimes difficult to determine which of these alternatives is the proper description; both are common in Greek laws.

b. A sanction may be followed by another sanction. In
this case the second sanction applies either (i) to
the case in which the first sanction is violated (e.g.,
"If a man kills another, he is exiled; if he does not
go into exile, he is executed.") or (ii) to a separate
though perhaps related case (e.g., "If a man kills
a free man, he is to pay *x*; if a man kills a slave, he is
to pay *y*."). Both these sequences are common in
Greek laws. The first is particularly common when
the sanction is a monetary fine, since provision is
often made for a further penalty in the case of non-
payment.

c. A regulation may be followed by a sanction. Most
commonly (i) the sanction applies to a violation of
the regulation (e.g., "He who will contend about
possession of a free man or a slave is not to seize the
man before trial; if he does seize him, he must pay
. . ."). Or (ii) the sanction may apply to a further
case, more or less closely related, which does not involve a specific violation of the regulation. At Gortyn (II.54–III.5), for example, if the husband declares
he is not the cause of the divorce, "the judge is to
decide the case on oath. If she carries off anything of
her husband's property, she shall pay him five staters
and return what she has taken." Here the second
provision, a sanction, concerns a related matter but
does not apply specifically to a violation of the
preceding regulation.

d. Finally, a sanction may be followed by a regulation.

This sequence is common, and as in the previous categories the regulation may apply either (i) to the case specified in the sanction or (ii) to a new case.

This elaboration of possible combinations of regulations and sanctions enables us to determine a rule concerning the use of καί and δέ as connectives in these situations. The rule is quite simple: in all cases δέ is the more common connective; in b(i), b(ii), and c(i) καί is never used; in a(i), a(ii), d(i), d(ii), and rarely in c(ii) καί may be used. In other words, whenever a sanction is joined to another sanction, or when a sanction follows a regulation and applies to a violation of that regulation, the sanction is connected by δέ to the preceding sanction or regulation.

The reason for this situation is evident if we consider the difference between καί and δέ. The former when it joins two clauses is normally copulative, equivalent to English "and" and sometimes as strong as "also" or "furthermore." On the other hand, δέ, in Denniston's words (*GP*, p. 162), "denotes either pure connexion, 'and,' or contrast, 'but,' with all that lies between." This intermediate range is significant for our purpose, for it is the intermediate sense of δέ (which we might translate "and/but") that accounts for its exclusive use in cases b(i), b(ii), and c(i).

Take, for instance, the case b(ii), of two successive independent sanctions (e.g., "If a man kills a free man, he is to pay x; if a man kills a slave, he is to pay y."). In one sense the second sanction is added to the first as in a series, and the appropriate connective would be a simple copulative. In another sense, however, there is always some difference between the offenses described in each of the two sanctions, and there is usually a difference in the penalties as well. Thus, an adversative connective which expressed this sense of contrast would also be appropriate. Since καί

can express only the first kind of connection it is not used
in such cases, and δέ is the regular connective.

The situation is well illustrated by the sanctions for
adultery at Gortyn (II.20–28), which I quote in Willetts's
translation: "If someone be taken in adultery with a
free woman in a father's, brother's or the husband's house,
he shall pay a hundred staters; but if [αἱ δέ] in another's
fifty; and if [αἱ δέ] with the wife of an *apetairos*, ten; but
if [αἱ δέ] a slave with a free woman, he shall pay double;
and if [αἱ δέ] a slave with a slave, five." This translation
makes it clear that in English, which has no word equivalent to this sense of δέ ("and/but"), the choice between
"and" and "but" in such cases is quite arbitrary. In Greek,
on the other hand, the need for this special kind of connection, both copulative and adversative, between two
successive sanctions requires that δέ be used and not καί.

In the other two cases in which καί is never found,
b(i) and c(i), the need for an adversative connective is even
stronger. In both these cases the second element is a
sanction applying to a violation of the requirement set
forth in the first element, whether a sanction or a regulation. Thus, there is always a contrast between the penalty or procedure set forth in the first provision and the
violation described in the protasis of the second provision.
Indeed, the protasis is often expressed as exactly the
negative of the action prescribed in the preceding provision
(e.g., "If a man . . . , he is to pay *x*; if he does not pay, he
is to. . . . ").[6]

This last observation leads to one final generalization:
it is clear that when the second provision in cases b(i),

6. Bloch, pp. 148–49, collects many examples of this type, in
most of which the connective is δέ; a few variations (primarily in
Plato's *Laws*) employ ἤ in the sense "or else."

b(ii), and c(i) specifies a violation that is described with a negative, the contrast between this violation and the preceding sanction or regulation is especially strong, and the connecting particle is regularly δέ. In fact no matter what the sequence of sanctions and regulations, καί is rarely used as the connective when the second provision begins with a negative protasis.

These generalizations about the use of καί and δέ as connectives in Greek laws are based on the evidence of surviving laws. In the absence of previous studies I have surveyed a large number of Greek laws preserved in inscriptions and in the text of the orators.[7] The results, presented below, are a classification of all examples I have found of καί εἰ; instances of εἰ δέ are too common to require comment.

The results of this investigation cannot constitute certain proof concerning Drakon's usage, since the survey is not exhaustive, and more important, we have no other Attic laws as early as Drakon's. The evidence is drawn from different parts of the Greek world and from laws written at different periods.[8] Two further difficulties are that

---

7. For the following survey I have examined all the laws preserved in the Attic orators, the laws at Gortyn in *IC* 4 (primarily from the "Great Code" [*IC* 4.72], hereafter referred to simply as "Gortyn"), and the laws in *IJG, GD, GHI, LS,* and *IGS* (for these abbreviations see above, pp. xi–xiii). I have included a number of texts of decrees, contracts, and the like which might not be considered laws in a strict sense.

8. On the whole, early Greek legal inscriptions show many of the same stylistic features as classical Greek prose; see Bloch, pp. 135–54. καί as a connective between main clauses seems to have become more common in later Greek prose (cf. G. Laminger-Pascher, *Index Grammaticus zu den griechischen Inschriften Kilikiens und Isauriens,* vol. 2, SB Wien 298.3 [1974]:122–23). Eduard Norden (*Agnostos Theos* [Leipzig, 1913], p. 367) and others

inscriptions are sometimes incomplete in crucial places, and
the laws in the orators may be quoted out of context or
in the wrong order.[9] Despite these difficulties there is such
consistent usage in all these laws, especially with regard to
the general rule above, that we are justified in assuming
with considerable confidence that the rule held also in Drakon's case.

The largest category consists of cases in which καὶ εἰ
introduces a regulation preceded by another regulation or
(less often) by a sanction (cases a(i), a(ii), d(i), d(ii)
above).[10] In such cases καὶ indicates that another regulation is being introduced which may continue the preceding context or introduce some new matter, but which
carries with it no sense of contrast with what precedes.
For example, the law requiring speakers to keep to the
point or be fined up to fifty drachmas (Ais. 1.35) stipulates

---

have attributed the large number of "καὶ-Sätze" in the New Testa-
ment to semitic influence, but S. Trenkner (*Le Style kai dans le récit
attique oral* [Assen, 1960]) argues for Attic influence.

9. There are certain discrepancies, for example, between the
order of the regulations in Drakon's law, lines 13–20, and the
quotation in Dem. 43.57. It is possible, however, that Demosthenes
is quoting from a different inscription, where the order was as he
gives it; see above, chap. 3, n. 66. Most of the laws found in the text
of the orators are now accepted as genuine; see N. M. Pusey,
"NOMOI ΤΩΝ ΑΘΗΝΑΙΩΝ" (Ph.D. diss., Harvard University,
1936), pp. 116–18; Louis Gernet, *Demosthène, Plaidoyers civils,* vol. 1
(Paris, 1954), pp. 21–22.

10. Dem. 23.60, 46.20; And. 1.97 (three times); Ais. 1.35;
Gortyn I.53, VIII.17, X.39; *IC* 4.81.16, 186.7, 186.10; *IJG* 4.41,
12.I.105, 12.I.127, 12.I.173, 13 (*bis*).24, 22.II.2, 22.III.16,
25.B.135; *GD* 4.C.4, 12.7, 19.25, 22.35, 27.50, 42.23, 67.27, 85.39;
GHI 45.4 (*bis*? see below, n. 20), 47.52, 65.13, 65.23, 70.20, 101.7–
8, 102.6–7, 118.28, 127.6, 136.18, 144.29, 151.9, 204.39; *LS* 13.27,
46.27, 46.29, 83.58, 83.61, 103.B.22.

that if a heavier fine is deserved, the case shall be referred
to the boule or the ekklesia, which will judge the case; "and
if (καὶ ἐάν) he is convicted" the proedroi are to certify the
fine for the collectors. In such cases καί has the general
sense "furthermore"; in some cases it is as strong as "also"
(e.g., *IJG* 25.B.135).[11] In some of these cases in which
the context is missing, we may infer a context of conti-
nuity without contrast.[12]

The other large category includes cases in which καὶ
εἰ introduces not a separate sentence but an additional provision within a sentence.[13] Of course sentence division in
Greek prose is to some extent a modern editorial decision,
but in all these cases there is a clear indication that the
conditional clause deals with the same matter or is directed
toward the same end as the preceding part of the sentence.
At Gortyn (III.29), for example, a childless widow is to keep
her own property and whatever she has woven and a share
of the estate's produce, "and if (καὶ) her husband gave

---

11. In treaties καὶ εἰ commonly introduces provisions for one
party which are exactly the same as the corresponding provisions previously set forth for the other party; see *GD* 85.39 and the references
to *GHI* 101–51 in the preceding note.

12. In Dem. 23.60 (= Drakon's law, lines 37–38) and Dem. 46.20
short regulations are quoted which begin with καὶ ἐάν. In the first
case it is likely that the law was closely connected to the clause that
immediately preceded it in line 37 on our stele (see above, chap. 3).
In the second case the wording of the law implies that it comes from
a context of laws dealing with *epikleroi*.

13. Gortyn III.29, VI.23, VI.43, IX.14; *IJG* 10.A.10, 24.VI.31,
24.VI.35, 24.VII.12, 28.D.12–15 (four times); *GD* 120.126; *GHI*
52.54, 58.A.11, 58.A.13, 58.A.26, 68.23, 69.31, 69.44, 85.46, 87.29
LS 36.10, 51.44, 51.135; *IGS*, p. 159. One slightly different case
should be noted here: the first example in Dem. 43.51, in which two
protases are joined by καί: "If there are brothers and if (καὶ ἐάν)
the brothers have sons, . . . "

her anything" [*sc.* she is to keep that, too].[14] In this example there is an obvious series of which the conditional clause is another member; in effect it is a noun clause functioning as an equivalent with, say, "gifts from her husband."

In other examples there are only two elements in the series: again at Gortyn (VI.23 = VI.43 = IX.14), an illegal mortgager is to repay double [the mortgage], and if (καὶ) there is any other (ἄλλα) damage [to the property], he shall pay the simple value. One might say that this sentence contains two separate sanctions, but it is clear from the context that the two sanctions are treated as part of one offense, namely illegal mortgaging. Here the close connection between the two parts is also indicated by ἄλλα in the second protasis; this is a common feature of the items in this category, and even when ἄλλος is not present, the sense of "whoever/whatever else" is implied, as in the example of the widow's property.

One or two instances of καὶ εἰ are found in category c(ii), a regulation followed by a sanction that does not specify a violation of the regulation.[15] It is significant that in the only certain example in this category (*GHI* 46.41)[16] the penalty is the same as in the preceding clause (τὰς γραφὰς εἶναι κατ' αὐτοῦ καὶ τὴν ζημίαν κατὰ ταὐτά), even though the sanction introduced by καὶ ἐάν is quite different and comes, in Meiggs-Lewis's words (p. 120), as

---

14. The sense of καί τι here (III.29) must be virtually the same as κᾱτι (= καὶ ὅτι, "and whatever") in III.20.

15. In *GHI* 45.8 καὶ ἐάν is restored by the editors of *ATL* (II.D.14) in a large gap (twenty-nine letters) in the only copy of this portion. The restoration is quite uncertain, and Meiggs-Lewis do not print any of it except καὶ ἐάν.

16. καί is restored in this case (*GHI* 46.41), but the gap is only twelve letters and the καί seems fairly certain.

"an unexpected digression." The use of καί here probably results from the fact that the penalty in this case is identical with the preceding penalty. καὶ ἐάν has a similar function in Dem. 59.16, though it does not begin the sentence. After sanctions and regulations governing intercourse between a male alien and a female citizen the law continues: ἔστω δὲ καὶ ἐὰν ἡ ξένη τῷ ἀστῷ συνοικῇ κατὰ ταὐτά ("and [δέ] let it be the same also if [καὶ ἐάν] a female alien has intercourse with a male citizen").

Two other examples in the largest category should be mentioned here, since in both cases καὶ εἰ introduces a clause that might be considered a sanction rather than a regulation. The first, a decree from Amphipolis (*GD* 12.7), declares that certain men "themselves and their children are to be exiled forever, and if (καὶ ἤν) they are caught any-where [in the territory], they will be treated as public enemies and may be killed with impunity." Here the regulation (or sanction) follows as a natural, almost automatic consequence of the initial declaration. Since it does not explicitly specify a violation of the declaration, there is no contrast felt between the declaration and the regulation that follows. The regulation could have been written as a sanction applying to a violation of the declaration— e.g., ". . . they are to be exiled forever; if they do not go into exile, they may be killed"— in which case the connecting particle would probably have had to be δέ.[17] The

_____

17. This example indicates how subtle the difference can be between cases in which καί is permitted and those in which δέ must be used because a contrast is felt. In English the difference is simi-lar: in my alternative version, for example (" . . . they are to be exiled forever; ——— if they do not go into exile, . . . "), most people prob-ably would supply "but" (the required sense may be closer to "and/but"), whereas my translation of the actual decree runs smoothly with "and." I treat the second element as expressed in the decree as

second example (*IJG* 22.III.16 = *RIG* 524) is similar; there is a close connection between the regulation introduced by καὶ ἐάν and what precedes, and the second element could be treated as a sanction.

The final category consists of a few cases in which καὶ εἰ means "even if."[18] In such cases καὶ does not function as a connective and usually does not introduce a separate provision but rather an additional clause within a provision. In only one of these does καὶ εἰ begin a sentence (see below), and of the rest, in all but one instance (*GD* 65.6) the clause introduced by καὶ εἰ ends a sentence. Of course, there is only a fine line between "also if" and "even if" (cf. German *auch wenn*), and certain examples classified under the largest category above might also be included here (e.g., *IJG* 12.I.127, 25.B.135).

Among all these examples of καὶ εἰ there are only three (or perhaps four) cases in which it is followed by μή. First, in the Heraklean tablets dealing with the use of certain sacred land (*IJG* 12 = *GD* 79) is a clause (table 1, lines 126–27) requiring that the names of those who plant trees and the number of trees be recorded, "and in the same way also [even?] if some have not planted (ἀν αὐτὰ δὲ τὰ καὶ εἴ τινές κα μὴ πεφυτεύκωντι) according to the agreement, they shall record [these]." In this case the two regulations entail essentially the same procedure, so that although the procedure is applied in cases that are nominally opposed (those who plant and those who do not), there is no contrast felt between the two regulations. Moreover, δέ provides a connection between the two regulations,

---

a regulation rather than a sanction, since "if they are caught" does not explicitly specify an offense; in my alternate version, however, an offense is explicitly specified.

18. Dem. 24.39 (= 24.71), 43.51 (second example); *IJG* 14.113, 15.A.32, 15.B.35; *GD* 65.6.

so that καί serves to add emphasis rather than provide
connection (cf. Dem. 59.16). Another example of a negative protasis occurs in a decree from Korope (*LS* 83.61)
in which καὶ εἰ joins two regulations in the form of conditional sentences; both have negative protases.

One or two other examples of καὶ εἰ μή may occur
near the beginning of the Athenian coinage decree (*GHI*
45.4). The preserved text begins with instructions for
the Athenian officials in various cities to publish the new
weights and measures; if they do not, they will be tried
and punished (45.1–2). But/and if (ἐὰν δέ) someone other
than the officials does not act in accordance with the
decree, he will be *atimos* and his property will be confiscated (45.3). "And if there are not ([καὶ εἰ μ]ή εἰσιν)
any Athenian officials, the officials of each city are to
carry out the provisions of the decree, and if they do
not act in accordance with the decree ([καὶ] ἐὰν μὴ ποιῶσι
κατὰ τ[ὰ ἐψηφισμένα]), let there be a prosecution of these
officials in Athens concerning a penalty of *atimia* (περὶ
[ἀτιμίας])" (45.4). Much of the text, including both instances of καί, is restored.[19]

The first καί joins one regulation to another, and
although the two cases—if there are Athenian officials in
the city and if there are not—are contraries, the treatment of the officials in the two cases is similar, and this

---

19. This part of the coinage decree is preserved in two copies,
from Kos and Aphytis, and the restorations (see *ATL* II.D.14) are
made on the basis of the stoichedon nature of both copies. The
first καί is restored in both copies. The restoration of the second
καί, however, seems possible only in the fragment from Kos; in
the fragment from Aphytis [ἐὰν δὲ μ]ὴ ποιῶσι is restored. If these
different restorations are both correct, then we cannot say which
connective was used in the original. This discrepancy may indicate
that the choice between καί and δέ in this case was felt to be arbitrary.

similarity accounts for the use of καί. The uncertainty of
the restoration makes me hesitate to accept the second καί,
which if genuine might be the only example of καί introducing a sanction that involves a violation of the preceding
regulation (i.e., c(i)). [20] If καί is genuine, it must have been
influenced (like the first καί) by the similarity of the treatment in cases in which there are and in which there are not
Athenian officials.

Of all these instances of καὶ εἰ there is only one that
occurs at the beginning of a legal text, [21] the decree of
Timokrates quoted in Dem. 24.39 and again in 24.71. In
both cases the quotation begins with a brief official pre-
amble ending with Τιμοκράτης εἶπε, followed directly by
the decree: καὶ εἴ τινι τῶν ὀφειλόντων τῷ δημοσίῳ προστετίμηται κατὰ νόμον ἢ κατὰ ψήφισμα δεσμοῦ ἢ τὸ λοιπὸν
προστιμηθῇ, εἶναι αὐτῷ ἢ ἄλλῳ ὑπὲρ ἐκείνου ἐγγυητὰς
καταστῆσαι τοῦ ὀφλήματος, κτλ., which I translate, omitting
καί for the moment and maintaining as closely as possible
the Greek word order: " . . . if any one of those in debt to
the state has been additionally sentenced according to a
law or a decree to prison or in the future will be additionally sentenced, it shall be allowed to him or to another on
his behalf to furnish sureties for his debt, etc." Translators
generally ignore the καί, but its genuineness seems guaranteed not only by the two quotations of the law inserted in the text but also by Demosthenes' repeated
references to the wording of the decree, including καί. [22]

---

20. The provision states that the officials should be tried in
Athens περὶ [ἀτιμίας]. It is difficult to determine whether this
should be classified as a regulation or a sanction.

21. In Dem. 23.60 it is certain, and in Dem. 46.20 very probable,
that the law quoted was originally preceded by other laws; see above,
n. 12.

22. Every time Demosthenes quotes the beginning of the decree,

What, then, is the force of this καί? Coming as it does
at the beginning of a decree, it cannot be a connecting
particle in the sense of "and, also, furthermore," but must
be used adverbially in the sense of "even"; but what is
the force of this "even"? If we insert "even" at the beginning of the translation above, can we determine what
particular aspect of the conditional clause is being emphasized by this initial adverb? "Even if any one of those in
debt to the state has been additionally sentenced according
to a law or a decree to prison or in the future will be additionally sentenced," he may provide sureties and thereby
remain out of jail for a time. The initial καί emphasizes the
special nature of this situation and implies that normally
a state debtor would not be additionally sentenced to prison and would thus stay out of jail in any event. Such was
indeed the case: most state debtors were only barred from
certain public functions until they paid their debt.[23] Timokrates' decree provides that *even* in cases in which a
state debtor is additionally sentenced to jail (whether in
the past or in the future), he or others on his behalf may
furnish sureties and remain free.[24] Thus, the initial καί
gives a special emphasis to the conditional clause. We shall
examine the implications of this emphasis in greater
detail in the next chapter.

---

he includes the καί (24.41, 44, 46, 72, 79, 93). See also the law that
Demosthenes ironically proposes in imitation of Timokrates' decree
(24.73); it too begins καὶ εἰ.

23. See, e.g., Harrison, vol. 2, pp. 243–44.

24. This interpretation of the καί at the beginning of Timokrates'
decree was suggested to me by Victor Bers. I had earlier followed
Demosthenes' discussion of the decree, in which he implies that the
καί emphasizes the retroactive nature of the decree as expressed
by the perfect tense, προστετίμηται (see, e.g., 24.44), but I now agree
with Bers that this interpretation "suits his rhetorical purpose and
cannot serve as an unbiased gloss on the law."

This survey of καὶ εἰ in Greek laws provides us with
several conclusions. First, it is not easy in some cases to
say exactly why καί is used and not δέ, but καί as a connective normally emphasizes the addition of a provision
when no contrast is felt with the preceding provision. On
the other hand, in cases in which there is a contrast, and
especially in the cases I have listed as b(i), b(ii), and c(i),
δέ is (with perhaps one exception) always used. Second,
καὶ εἰ μή is particularly rare for the obvious reason that a
negative protasis usually indicates a contrast with the preceding provision. Third, καὶ εἰ in the sense "even if" is
rare and usually introduces the final clause in the sentence.
However, in the only example (other than Drakon's law)
of καὶ εἰ at the beginning of a legal document, it has the
sense "even if" and serves to emphasize that the decree
applies to certain exceptional situations.

καὶ ἐάν AT THE BEGINNING OF DRAKON'S LAW

With the survey of καὶ εἰ in Greek legal writings as our basis, we may now examine καὶ ἐάν at the beginning of Drakon's law. First we shall consider the common hypothesis that καί originally joined the law on unintentional homicide to a preceding law on intentional homicide, and shall try to determine under what conditions, if any, this would have been possible. We shall then consider the possibility that καί originally began Drakon's homicide law and shall try to determine what the force of καί would be in this case and why Drakon might have begun his law in this way.

In view of our conclusions in the last chapter, it seems almost impossible that καί could have been used to connect the existing law on unintentional homicide to the sort of provision concerning intentional homicide which is usually suggested. Certainly Gilbert's suggestion, ἐὰν ἐκ προνοίας κτείνῃ τίς τινα, ἀποθανεῖν ἢ φεύγειν καὶ τὰ ἐκείνου ἄτιμα εἶναι· καὶ ἐὰν μὴ ἐκ προνοίας . . . , or Ruschenbusch's ἐὰν ἐκ προνοίας κτείνῃ τίς τινα, χρῆσθαι αὐτῷ ὅπως ἂν ἐθέλῃ, τὰ δὲ χρήματα αὐτοῦ ἄτιμα εἶναι, καὶ ἐὰν μὴ ἐκ προνοίας . . . ,[1] would be unparalleled in the use of καί. In these examples the connective would almost certainly have had to be δέ, since in both there is a definite contrast

---

1. Gustav Gilbert, *Jahrbücher für classische Philologie* Supplement 23 (1897), pp. 490, 514. Ruschenbusch, "*phonos*," p. 145, n. 74.

between the two laws. Even if the law on intentional homicide was longer and included a number of regulations in addition to a statement of the sanction, it is hard to imagine how these regulations could have been written so that the transition to the law on unintentional homicide by means of the connective καί would have been possible. The law on intentional homicide must in that case have been presented as a separate law from that on unintentional homicide, and in view of the clear contrast between the two offenses, emphasized by the fact that one is expressed as the negative of the other, the connection between them would have to be provided by δέ.

The only circumstance under which καί might be used as a connective between these two laws is if the stated penalty in both laws was the same: if, in other words, the penalty for intentional homicide in Drakon's law was exile, and not death as is almost universally assumed.[2] In this case καί might perhaps be the connective: ἐὰν ἐκ προνοίας κτείνῃ τίς τινα, φεύγειν, καὶ ἐὰν μὴ ἐκ προνοίας κτείνῃ τίς τινα, φεύγειν. There is no parallel for this use of καί to join two sanctions,[3] and the repetition seems flat, to say the least, but such an expression might not be impossible. One might in this case, however, expect a more concise statement, perhaps simply ἐὰν κτείνῃ τίς τινα, φεύγειν or, more fully, ἐὰν ἐκ προνοίας καὶ ἐὰν μὴ ἐκ

---

2. Gilbert's suggestion includes exile as one of the penalties for intentional homicide, but only Maschke (p. 46) has suggested (in passing) that the penalty for intentional homicide was fully the same as for unintentional homicide. He reached this conclusion on the basis of the implication of καὶ ἐάν in the sense "even if" (see below, n. 14). For a discussion of the penalty for intentional homicide see below, chap. 7.

3. The closest parallel would be the regulations on planting trees in *IJG* 12.I.126–27, but there the actual connection is provided by a δέ (see above, pp. 91–92).

προνοίας κτείνῃ τίς τινα, φεύγειν. Or if one wanted to emphasize the inclusion of unintentional homicide in the law, one might use καί in the sense of "even" and write, e.g., ἐὰν κτείνῃ τίς τινα, καὶ ἐὰν μὴ ἐκ προνοίας, φεύγειν. We shall return to these possibilities later.

In sum, in view of other uses of καὶ εἰ it is difficult to reconstruct a law on intentional homicide preceding the preserved law on unintentional homicide which would account for their being connected by καί. Only if the penalty was the same in both cases would such a connective be possible. We must thus consider the alternative, that καὶ ἐάν originally began the law.

If καί originally stood at the beginning of Drakon's law, as it does now, it must have been used adverbially in the sense of "even." Before asking what force καί might have had in this case, we must consider briefly the general use of adverbial καί at the beginning of conditional clauses.

Adverbial καί normally adds emphasis to the word or words immediately following it. When a conditional clause is emphasized by καί, the adverb implies (like the English "even if") that the condition is somehow a special case, usually a more remote or more extreme possibility. Furthermore, the situation in a conditional clause introduced by καὶ εἰ is always by implication contrasted with another situation in some way its contrary, which (it is implied) is more probable or more common or more expected.[4] Thus, when

---

4. Denniston (*GP*, pp. 299–305, 584–85) is most concerned with the difference between καὶ εἰ and εἰ καί, and his discussion is not very helpful for our purpose; from the context in Drakon's law it is clear that καὶ ἐάν does not introduce an admitted fact ("even though") but rather a true condition. Kühner-Gerth (II.2.488) say that a condition introduced by καὶ εἰ in the sense of "auch wenn, sogar wenn" is thereby designated "unmöglich oder unwahrscheinlich." In their example (καὶ εἰ ἀθάνατος ἦν), however, the

Athena tells Odysseus (*Od.* 13.291–92) that it would be
difficult for anyone to surpass him in treachery "even if a
god should contest against you" (καὶ εἰ θεὸς ἀντιάσειε),
she implies that this is an extreme case and that of course
it would also be difficult for another mortal to surpass
him in treachery.

Here it is obvious from the context and from the common opposition of god and mortal that the implied contrary of "even if a god should contest against you" is "if a
mortal should contest against you." In other cases the
implied contrary is simply the negative of the condition,
and generally the verb or some other important word in
the conditional clause has an obvious contrary. Isokrates
(4.28), for instance, before beginning to tell the story
of Demeter at Eleusis comments, "Even if the story has become a myth (καὶ γὰρ εἰ μυθώδης ὁ λόγος γέγονεν), it is
fitting nonetheless that it be retold now." Isokrates implies
that if the story were not a myth (that is, if it were true),
it would certainly be fitting that it be retold. The implication of this and other examples of conditional sentences
beginning with καὶ εἰ[5] is that the conclusion in the apodosis
is also valid, and usually more obviously valid, when the
contrary condition holds.

Let us now turn to the beginning of Drakon's law. If
the law originally began with καί in the adverbial sense of
"even," we obviously must understand the implied contrary of "even if a man not intentionally kills another"
to be the more common possibility "if a man intentionally
kills another." Whether or not this more common alterna-

---

impossibility of the condition is expressed by the syntax (counter-
factual condition) rather than by the introductory καί. Nonetheless, in general καὶ εἰ does suggest that there is at least a degree of
improbability to the condition.
5. See, e.g., Eur. *Med.* 463, Ar. *Wasps* 813, Sappho 1.21.

tive has been explicitly stated, its existence is implicitly
assumed by the clause beginning with "even if."

A further implication is that the penalty for the more
common case, intentional homicide, is the same as the
penalty for the more remote case, unintentional homicide.
This implication is perhaps less evident if we think in
terms of English "even if," for it may be possible in English
to say, "If a man intentionally kills another, he is executed;
even if a man does not intentionally kill another, he is
exiled." It does not seem possible in Greek, however, to
write, ἐὰν ἐκ προνοίας κτείνῃ τίς τινα, ἀποθανεῖν · καὶ ἐὰν
μὴ ἐκ προνοίας κτείνῃ τίς τινα, φεύγειν. This is precisely
the wording we rejected above on the ground that there is
a clear contrast between the two provisions and thus δέ,
not καί, must be the connective.

The underlying principle here is that the sense "even"
for καί is in fact an extension of the sense "also." As
Denniston notes (GP, p. 293), "Greek does not, like English, express the distinction between these two ideas."
Thus, in Greek one cannot use καί in the sense of "even"
when the sense "and also" would not also be suitable
to connect the more unusual case with the (expressed or
unexpressed) more common case. The examples discussed
above and in the preceding chapter all support this conclusion: when καὶ εἰ introduces a conditional sentence
whose conclusion in the apodosis is valid for a certain more
extreme or more remote case, the same conclusion must
also be valid for the more common case, whether or not it
is explicitly stated. Thus Drakon could not have written
καὶ ἐὰν μὴ ἐκ προνοίας κτείνῃ τίς τινα, φεύγειν if the penalty for the more common case, intentional homicide,
was not also exile—whether or not this more common case
was explicitly stated.

In sum, if Drakon's law originally began just as it does

in the preserved copy, καὶ ἐὰν μὴ ἐκ προνοίας κτείνῃ τίς
τινα, φεύγειν, then this provision would in itself imply that
of course if the killing is intentional, the killer is also
exiled. This is the only possibility that is fully consistent
with the use of καὶ εἰ elsewhere.

The question remains, however, if we accept the
conclusion that καὶ originally began Drakon's law, must we
also accept Stroud's theory that the law on intentional
homicide came later in the law? We have already examined
a number of serious difficulties with this theory, and thus
I am led to suggest a different solution to the problem of
the law on intentional homicide, a solution that raises its
own difficulties but may nonetheless be more convincing
than the alternatives.

My suggestion is that we should understand the first
sentence of Drakon's law, which treats unintentional homicide explicitly and intentional homicide by implication,
to be the basic statement of the law on all homicide, intentional and unintentional. In other words, Drakon wrote
no separate law on intentional homicide, but by beginning
his law with the statement "Even if a man not intentionally kills another, he is exiled" he meant to state the law
on all homicide, on intentional homicide by implication
and on unintentional homicide explicitly, just as I might tell
a class before an examination, "Even if someone unintentionally looks at another student's paper, he will fail the
examination," thereby clearly implying that the same penalty will apply to anyone who intentionally looks at
another's paper.

That the opening sentence of Drakon's law carries this
implication is in my view probable. On the other hand,
that Drakon actually wrote his homicide law in such
an elliptical manner may strike some as improbable. In
the remainder of this chapter I shall offer some further

considerations in support of this hypothesis and shall then
evaluate it in comparison with the other proposed theories
concerning Drakon's law on intentional homicide.

The first question we must ask is, would the implication that Drakon's first sentence also covers intentional
homicide truly be clear to his readers? Certainly it is possible to imagine expressions beginning with καὶ εἰ or "even
if" in which the sense is not immediately clear (see below
on Timokrates' decree), but it also is easy to suggest
examples in which the sense is evident (see above on *Od.*
13.291–92 and Isok. 4.28). Consider, for instance, a
sign in the door of a china shop which reads, "Even if you
unintentionally break something in this store, you must
pay for it." Certainly this implies that a similar penalty will
be in effect for intentionally breaking something in the
store.

The reasons for the unambiguous nature of this and
the other examples cited above are threefold. First, the
particular word which expresses the extreme nature of the
case and which is emphasized by καὶ or "even" (e.g., "unintentionally") comes at or near the beginning of the conditional clause; thus it is clear that this is the emphasized
word. Second, "unintentionally," because it has a single,
obvious contrary, clearly indicates what the more common,
unexpressed situation is. And third, from our general
familiarity with the situation, we would expect or at least
not be surprised by a similar penalty in the more common case. If anything, it is the expressed situation which
might surprise us; in other words, we expect to pay for
intentional damage, but we might expect not to have to
pay for something broken unintentionally.

Besides Drakon's law the only other example of καὶ εἰ
beginning a Greek legal text is found in Timokrates'
decree (Dem. 24.39; see above, pp. 93–94), which begins
καὶ εἴ τινι τῶν ὀφειλόντων τῷ δημοσίῳ προστετίμηται

κατὰ νόμον ἢ κατὰ ψήφισμα δεσμοῦ ἢ τὸ λοιπὸν προστιμηθῇ
. . . As we saw, without a context to guide us the force of
καί is not immediately clear and Demosthenes seems to mis-
represent it in his attack on the decree.[6] All three features
which might clarify the matter are missing: the verbs, προστετίμηται and προστιμηθῇ, do not stand at the beginning
of the clause;[7] the contrary of the clause (in this case simply
its negation, "if someone has not been and will not be additionally sentenced to prison") is not immediately certain;
and for us, at least, the general background of the decree
may be unclear. But despite this lack of clarity, καὶ εἰ at the
beginning of Timokrates' decree functions just as it does in
the other cases I have cited: it stresses the exceptional nature
of the condition being introduced and confirms by implication the validity of the contrary conditional statement.

Unlike the beginning of Timokrates' decree, the opening sentence of Drakon's law is quite clear in its implications. This sentence certainly satisfies the first two criteria
noted above: the emphasized phrase, μὴ ἐκ προνοίας,
stands first in the conditional clause after ἐάν, and the expression has a single, obvious contrary, ἐκ προνοίας. Indeed, I suggest that the rare expression μὴ ἐκ προνοίας (see
above, pp. 35–36) is employed here by Drakon instead of
the more common ἄκων precisely in order to make un-
equivocally clear the unexpressed, more common situation, homicide ἐκ προνοίας. Drakon could have used ἄκων
with the contrary ἐκών (or ἐκ προνοίας) implied, but μὴ
ἐκ προνοίας makes his point even clearer.

---

6. See above, chap. 5, n. 24.

7. We should note that when Demosthenes repeats the opening
of Timokrates' decree in order to discuss its implications, he quickly
reduces the conditional clause to καὶ εἴ τινι προστετίμηται (24.44)
in order to bring out more emphatically the force of the καί as he
interprets it—i.e., as emphasizing the perfect tense of the verb.

The third factor, the general background of Drakon's
law, is more difficult for us to assess. From our earlier discussion of pre-Drakontian homicide law (above, Chapter
Two), however, it seems likely that the most common penalty for homicide was exile, though occasionally death
might result. Moreover, though almost all the homicides
mentioned in the epic poems are to our knowledge intentional, it seems clear from one example, Odysseus's killing
of Antinoos, that an unintentional homicide would be
treated in the same way as an intentional homicide. It thus
seems likely that the proper context did exist for understanding that the opening sentence of Drakon's law applies
by implication also to intentional homicide. If homicide—
which in most cases meant intentional homicide—traditionally led to the killer's exile, then when Drakon began his
law "Even if a man not intentionally kills another, he
is exiled," the reader would easily understand the implication that in the more common case of intentional homicide the penalty was also exile.

In this view, Drakon wrote his law in such a way as to
emphasize the penalty for unintentional homicide. This
indicates that there probably was a growing movement to
treat unintentional homicide separately from intentional
homicide and perhaps to reduce the penalties for it. In such
a situation Drakon may have felt the need to emphasize
that unintentional homicide would also be punished with
exile, just as intentional homicide commonly was. Thus,
by beginning his law καὶ ἐὰν μὴ ἐκ προνοίας κτείνῃ τίς τινα,
φεύγειν, Drakon was conservatively resisting a trend to
greater leniency. If this interpretation is correct, it accords
well with Drakon's later reputation for severity (see below,
Chapter Seven).

I have argued that the first words of the preserved
fragment were also the first words of the law in its original
form. It is possible, however, that these were not the first

words on the original axon, just as they are not the first words on the preserved stele. We have no way of knowing for certain, but it is possible that at the beginning of his law on homicide Drakon gave an indication of the subject matter in the form of a heading or title.[8]

If Drakon gave his law a heading, we can perhaps conjecture what it was on the basis of the preserved decree providing for the re-publication of τὸν Δράκοντος νόμον τὸν περὶ τοῦ φόνου. It is certain that νόμος was not on the original inscription, since we know that Drakon referred to his law as a θεσμός (line 20),[9] and thus the first four words of this label are apparently not original. The last words, however, περὶ τοῦ φόνου, might easily have stood at the head of the law, or perhaps simply the genitive φόνου.[10] Either expression would have provided a clear, simple heading. Of course it is merely speculation that Drakon's law originally had a heading, but the presence of φόνου or περὶ τοῦ φόνου at the beginning would make even clearer the force of the first words of the law, since the heading would indicate that the context for the opening statement was homicide in general.

The word φόνος, moreover, is a less neutral term than

---

8. The designation πρῶτος ἄξων may also have been inscribed at the head of Drakon's axon, as it is on the stele. If so, it could have come either before or after a title (if there was one).

9. See Stroud, p. 20, and M. Ostwald, *Nomos and the Beginnings of the Athenian Democracy* (Oxford, 1969), pp. 3–5.

10. From the presence of an initial genitive at the head of two of Solon's laws (F36, ἐξούλης; F70, ἀτίμων) Ruschenbusch (*SN*, p. 24) has conjectured that the titles of some of Solon's laws were simple genitives (for others a relative clause may have served as a title). For our purposes it makes little difference whether φόνου or περὶ τοῦ φόνου was the original title of Drakon's law, since the message conveyed to the reader of the law would be the same in either case.

"homicide." Although in some cases φόνος may designate homicide in general, it also commonly implies intentional killing, even without any qualification such as ἐκ προνοίας.[11] The law stating the jurisdiction of the Areopagos (Dem. 23.22), for example, mentions simply φόνου,[12] and the titles of Antiphon's tetralogies indicate that φόνος alone designates intentional homicide (*Tetr.* 1 and 3), whereas the case of unintentional homicide (*Tetr.* 2) is entitled φόνος ἀκούσιος. These and many other examples[13]

---

11. If φόνος is etymologically related to θείνω (see Hjalmar Frisk, *Griechisches etymologisches Wörterbuch* s.v. φόνος), it originally referred to killing with a blow and presumably implied intentional homicide.

12. In the expression φόνου καὶ τραύματος ἐκ προνοίας καὶ πυρκαῖας καὶ φαρμάκων (Dem. 23.22), some (e.g., MacDowell, p. 45) take ἐκ προνοίας with φόνου as well as with τραύματος. But the word order suggests rather that φόνου (like πυρκαῖας and φαρμάκων) alone designates the crime, which is intentional homicide, just as πυρκαῖας apparently means "arson," also by implication an intentional act; and Demosthenes' later reference to this law (23.67) confirms this: ἐν Ἀρείῳ πάγῳ, οὗ δίδωσιν ὁ νόμος καὶ κελεύει τοῦ φόνου δικάζεσθαι. In his discussion of the jurisdiction of the Areopagos (23.65-70) Demosthenes refers to δίκαι φόνου, φονικαὶ δίκαι, and the like with no explicit mention of intent. The fact that Aristotle (*Ath. Pol.* 57.3) rewords the law to make it explicitly designate homicide ἐκ προνοίας (ἂν μὲν ἐκ προνοίας ἀποκτείνῃ ἢ τρώσῃ) indicates only that from his more systematic point of view the unqualified φόνος of the original law needed qualification. Pollux (8.117) retains Demosthenes' wording and also speaks of φόνου in connection with the Areopagos but of τῶν ἀκουσίων φόνων in connection with the Palladion (8.118). The addition of ἐκ προνοίας to τραύματος may be intended to indicate that the crime is not simply intentional wounding but wounding with intent to kill; see above, p. 33.

13. E.g., Ant. 4.2.5; Dem. 20.157, 23.51, 54.18, 54.25; Lys. 1.30, 10.11, 26.12; Plato, *Laws* 866B1; Hesych. s.v. δικαστηρία.

show that an Athenian who read the heading φόνου (or
perhaps περὶ τοῦ φόνου) would expect a law primarily about
intentional homicide. Thus, if Drakon began his law
Φόνου. καὶ ἐὰν μὴ ἐκ προνοίας κτείνῃ τίς τινα, φεύγειν
(which we might translate "[The Law on] Murder:
"Even if a man not intentionally kills another, he is
exiled"), it would be immediately clear that this law
and the provisions that follow apply not only to the more
remote case, unintentional homicide, but also to the
more common one, intentional homicide (φόνος). In short,
the reader would know he was reading not Drakon's law
περὶ φόνου μὴ ἐκ προνοίας, but Drakon's law περὶ τοῦ φόνου.

Before proceeding further, we must consider an
objection that may be raised at this point: if this sense of
the law was so clear to Drakon and his readers, why have
modern readers for the most part overlooked it?[14] There
are three main reasons. First, scholars have generally
assumed that the homicide laws must have been substantially revised between Drakon's time and their re-publication
in 409/8, and that καὶ ἐάν was thus not the original beginning of the law. We have already seen, however, that revision
by amendment could have occurred without altering the
original wording of the law (see above, Chapter Two), and
that καὶ ἐάν may well have been the original beginning
of the law. Second, almost everyone has assumed that the
penalty for intentional homicide in Drakon's time was

---

14. Maschke (p. 46) did understand that καί in the sense of
"even" implies that the penalty for intentional homicide is the same
as that for unintentional homicide, but he considered the preserved
copy of the law to be so thoroughly interpolated that he never tried
to understand the preserved fragment as a whole. Recently K. Tsantsanoglou (ΚΕΡΝΟΣ [Thessalonika, 1972], pp. 170–79, 250) has
also concluded that this must be the implication of καὶ ἐάν, but since
he assumes that exile could not have been the regular penalty for
intentional homicide, he concludes that the first sentence in the law
(line 11) must be supplemented differently; see above, chap. 3, n. 1.

death. We shall consider this point in greater detail in
Chapter Seven, but our examination of the use of καὶ εἰ in
legal writing has shown that its use here is strong evidence
that the penalty for both kinds of homicide was the same,
whether or not καί originally began the law. Third, modern
law makes a sharper distinction between intentional and
unintentional homicide than was apparently the case in
Drakon's time, and this has led scholars to assume that
there must have been separate laws for the two different
offenses.

It is clear, then, that modern scholars have approached
Drakon's law with assumptions different from those of
an Athenian of Drakon's time (or even of the fourth century), and it thus may not be surprising that they have
misunderstood his meaning.

We may also ask, why did Drakon begin his homicide
law in such an elliptical manner when he could have made
his intent clearer by giving a fuller version of the law? To
answer this objection we can only speculate that Drakon
may have been seeking a concise and emphatic opening
statement. A terse, elliptical style is common in early laws,[15]
and we shall see (below, Chapter Eight) that in several
places Drakon omits details that must be inferred by the
reader. Thus, it is consistent with the style of the rest
of his law that it begins with the elliptical opening statement which has been preserved on the stele.

Proper evaluation of this hypothesis requires a comparison with the three theories concerning the law on
intentional homicide discussed in Chapter Four and a re-
view of the objections to each. First, Busolt-Swoboda
suggested that Drakon wrote no law on intentional homi-

---

15. See, e.g., the Elean *rhetra* (below, pp. 159–60), and cf.
J. Wackernagel, *Vorlesungen über Syntax*, vol. 1 (Basel, 1920), pp.
111–12.

cide but added his law on unintentional and lawful homicide to an already existing law. The major objection to this
theory is that even if Drakon did not write it, the law on
intentional homicide was considered his in the fifth century
and should have been re-published on the stele in 409/8
along with the rest of the law in accordance with the preserved decree.

This same objection also holds for the second theory,
that Drakon's law on intentional homicide originally
preceded the existing law but was not re-published with it.
Even a revised law on intentional homicide should have
been re-published on the stele. Another objection to this
view is that the initial καί should not have been retained
at the beginning of the law when it no longer had any function. Furthermore, καί should not have been used in the
first place to connect the law on intentional homicide to a
law on unintentional homicide, unless the penalty in both
cases was the same.

Third, Stroud's view that the law on intentional homicide originally stood later in the law meets with many
objections: that such an arrangement of provisions is unlikely, that it would require considerable repetition or
cross-reference, that several provisions (especially those
concerning the planner of a homicide, pardon, protection for the exiled killer, and self-defense) imply that the
law on intentional homicide has already been stated, and
that the force of the initial καί is still unexplained.

The hypothesis I have proposed is that the law on intentional homicide is implicitly included in the opening sentence, which in fact is a law on all homicide, not simply
unintentional homicide. In this view, Drakon's law on homicide was re-published in 409/8 just as it stood on the
original axones, and the re-published version preserves the
original arrangement of the law, which was clear, orderly,
and purposeful. The main difficulty with this theory is that

the ellipsis in the opening sentence is extreme and, as far as I know, unparalleled.[16] Even if the implications of the opening sentence are clear, it may seem unlikely that Drakon would have written his law in this way.

Nonetheless, I believe my hypothesis presents significantly less difficulty than the others. Certainty about the matter will probably never be possible without new evidence; for the moment, however, I maintain that this hypothesis provides both the best explanation for the preservation of Drakon's law in its present form on the stele and the most satisfactory basis for understanding the law as a whole.

If this hypothesis proves unpersuasive, the next best solution may be one that draws on two other theories as follows: assume that Drakon began his law with a brief statement of the law on intentional homicide, perhaps as brief as ἐὰν ἐκ προνοίας καὶ ἐὰν μὴ ἐκ προνοίας κτείνῃ τίς τινα, φεύγειν; that the law on intentional homicide was later revised and the opening words (ἐὰν ἐκ προνοίας) deleted; and that the revised provisions on intentional homicide were then added to the end of Drakon's law. These circumstances might account for the use of καί as a connective at the beginning of the law and would eliminate the problem of the law on intentional homicide's not being re-published on the stele in 409/8. The objections to this solution are that καί should have been deleted along with the initial three words, and that the resulting order of the provisions would still leave the revised version of the law with most of the difficulties that attend Stroud's theory.

---

16. The scarcity of inscriptional evidence for early laws or for any Attic documents before the fifth century may perhaps make the absence of an exact parallel less surprising. On ellipsis in early laws see preceding note.

THE TREATMENT OF INTENTIONAL HOMICIDE IN DRAKON'S LAW

Examination of the use of καὶ εἰ together with other considerations has led to the conclusion that intentional and unintentional homicide received basically the same treatment in Drakon's law. Certain minor features were different, such as the possibility of pardon when no relatives survived, but the important features—exile as the penalty, trial by the Ephetai, and the possibility of pardon when the relatives did survive—were the same for intentional and unintentional homicide under Drakon.

This conclusion runs counter to the prevailing scholarly opinion. Two assumptions in particular about the treatment of homicide in Drakon's time are common and, if correct, would be serious obstacles to our interpretation of the law; these are, first, that the penalty for intentional homicide was death, and second (though there is less agreement on this point), that cases of intentional homicide were tried at the Areopagos. There is no direct evidence for either of these assumptions, but since homicide seems to have been so treated in the fourth century in Athens, it is arguable that it was similarly treated in Drakon's original law, which the Attic orators claimed the city was still using. I shall consider each of these assumptions in turn.

With few exceptions[1] scholars hold that the penalty for

---

1. See above, chap. 6, n. 2. Ruschenbusch, who believes that intentional homicide was left to self-help in Drakon's law, must of course conclude that the death penalty was instituted only after Drakon's time ("*phonos,*" pp. 138–39).

intentional homicide in Drakon's time was death, not
exile. This view rests on the unanimous understanding that
the penalty for intentional homicide in the fourth century was death, but if we examine this assumption carefully
we shall find that it needs at least to be modified.

In a passage in which he is seeking to emphasize the
wickedness of intentional as opposed to unintentional in-
juries, Demosthenes (21.43) draws a sharp distinction
between the penalties for intentional and unintentional
homicide: "The homicide laws punish intentional killers
with death and perpetual exile and confiscation of property (θανάτῳ καὶ ἀειφυγίᾳ καὶ δημεύσει τῶν ὑπαρχόντων),
but they deem unintentional killers deserving of pardon
(αἰδέσεως) and charitable treatment." For our purposes
we may ignore the penalty of confiscation, which could
be imposed in addition to either death or exile.[2] We are
left, however, with two mutually exclusive penalties for
intentional homicide, death and exile. What was the relation between them?

We know that an accused killer could choose exile at
any time before his second speech at his trial.[3] The question
is, were death and exile regarded as two equivalent penalties for intentional homicide, or was exile considered something different, a means of avoiding, rather than paying,
the penalty for one's act? The common (though often un-
stated) assumption is that death was the true penalty for
intentional homicide and that exile was in effect a com-
muted death sentence.[4] The wording of Demosthenes'

---

2. See MacDowell, pp. 115–17.

3. Dem. 23.69; Ant. 4.4.1, 5.13 (cf. Ant. 2.2.9); Pollux 8.117.

4. See, e.g., Harrison, vol. 1, p. 198: "The penalty [for intentionally killing a citizen] was death, which, however, could be con-
verted into banishment for life if the defendant fled the country
before the end of the trial."

assertion in 21.43, however, which is the only direct statement we have of the penalty for intentional homicide,
implies rather that death and exile were both considered
penalties for intentional homicide. Moreover, Demosthenes is emphasizing the severity of the penalty for intentional homicide[5] and would probably have omitted any
mention of exile if it were not considered a true and severe
penalty.

There is some evidence in the orators that death was
the penalty for intentional homicide, but none of it com-
pels us to believe that it was the only penalty. For instance,
prosecutors in homicide cases sometimes ask the jury to
condemn the accused to death;[6] moreover, the defendant
in the Herodes homicide trial states that "the law is that
the killer is put to death" (Ant. 5.10), but since he is trying to draw as sharp a contrast as possible between the
regular procedure in homicide cases (the δίκη φόνου), in
which death may be the penalty, and the unusual procedure
in his case (*apagoge*), in which the penalty is to be assessed
by the court, he would be expected to emphasize a single
penalty for homicide.

The death penalty for homicide may also be implied
when Demosthenes says (23.69) that the prosecutor may
observe the convicted killer "paying the penalty established by law" (διδόντα δίκην ἣν ἔταξεν ὁ νόμος). Mac-
Dowell (p. 111) takes this to be a "euphemistic expression
for execution," and he may be right, but Demosthenes'

---

5. MacDowell notes (p. 117) that Demosthenes' statement in
21.43 of the penalty for unintentional homicide ("pardon and
charitable treatment") is "an over-lenient account of it." In fact
Demosthenes' words are quite misleading, since exile was the
explicit penalty for unintentional homicide (Dem. 23.72–73), though
pardon was possible.

6. E.g., Ant. 1.25–27, 4.1.7.

indirectness may also be a result of his desire not to exclude exile as a possible penalty even though he is thinking primarily of death. In sum, none of these passages is inconsistent with the possibility that exile was equally a penalty for intentional homicide. [7]

Two other passages in the orators imply that the penalty for intentional homicide was exile. In one Demosthenes (23.77–78) describes the odd procedure of the court "in Phreatto," in which a previously exiled killer approaches the shore in a boat and makes his plea in a new homicide case while the court listens from the shore. If he is convicted, says Demosthenes, "he pays the penalty for intentional homicide" (τὴν ἐπὶ τοῖς ἑκουσίοις φόνοις δίκην ἔδωκε). In view of the circumstances of the trial it seems unlikely that the court could execute anyone in such cases; most likely it would sentence the killer to perpetual exile. Moreover, earlier in the same speech (23.53) Demosthenes quotes a provision on lawful homicide that stipulates a number of specific situations (such as killing an adulterer) in which the killer "shall not be exiled" (τούτων ἕνεκα μὴ φεύγειν κτείναντα). [8] The clear implication of this law is that exile would otherwise be the penalty for the homicide.

---

7. The speaker in Lys. 6.14 says that in the Areopagos one who confesses to his crime is put to death, whereas one who contests the charge may be acquitted. If this refers to a charge of intentional homicide, it is certainly misleading, since many who were ready to confess to the deed must have gone into exile before being convicted. Cf. also *Dikon Onomata* s.v. φονικόν (= *Anecdota Bekker,* vol. 1, p. 194, quoted by Harrison, vol. 1, p. 198, n. 1), where the penalty for killing a citizen is said to be death.

8. It has been suggested (see Cantarella, p. 131, n. 2) that φεύγειν here may mean "stand trial." There are two objections to this suggestion: first, in all cases cited by LSJ (s.v. φεύγω IV) in which the verb means "stand trial" it occurs in a context that makes this sense clear, often with some clarifying phrase stating the charge

This evidence from the orators can best be explained by the assumption that death and exile were both considered penalties for intentional homicide, as stated by Demosthenes (21.43).[9] In accordance with rhetorical necessity the speaker might emphasize the death penalty or exile, or he might make an ambiguous reference to "the penalty for homicide." On the basis of our scanty evidence, exile seems to have been by far the more common penalty in homicide cases; to my knowledge there are no attested instances of someone's being executed after a δίκη φόνου.[10] Capital punishment was common in Athens for a number of "public" crimes[11] but was very rare otherwise, and it is likely that most of those who were in real danger of being convicted and sentenced to death in homicide cases went into exile first.[12] In sum, in the fourth century the penalty for intentional homicide was death and exile, more frequently the latter. Exile was a means of paying, not of avoiding, the penalty for one's crime.[13]

---

or penalty; and second (as Cantarella herself notes), those accused of lawful homicide did in fact stand trial, at least if the case was disputed, in the court at the Delphinion.

9. See also Ant. 2.2.9, where death and exile seem to be equally possible penalties in case of conviction.

10. Menestratos (Lys. 13.56) was executed for homicide, but he was tried by *apagoge* (MacDowell, pp. 137–38, Hansen, p. 130), his was clearly a political crime, and he was convicted by the boule under extraordinary circumstances.

11. By "public" I mean a crime that directly harms the state or a public institution (e.g., treason or selling contraband goods), as opposed to a "private" crime, which harms an individual but is seen (by us at least) as indirectly harming society (e.g., homicide).

12. Surely in some of these cases the accused would then be acquitted. MacDowell (p. 115) accepts too readily the statement in And. 1.3, which must be understood in its rhetorical context.

13. I have not used the evidence of the homicide law laid down by Athens for the Erythraians in the mid-fifth century, which seems

Turning now to Drakon's own time, we must first consider the tradition, best known from Plutarch (*Sol.* 17),[14] of the proverbial severity of Drakon's laws: "One penalty was assigned for nearly all offenses, namely death. . . . Those who stole vegetables or fruit were punished in the same way as temple robbers and killers (ἀνδροφόνοι)." This tradition was widespread and gave rise to puns on Drakon's name and to other witty remarks. For our purposes the question is, what historical basis was there to this tradition?

The tradition of Drakon's severity is first attested in the fourth century.[15] At this time it is likely that none of Drakon's laws survived except the law on homicide, the others having been superseded by the laws of Solon (*Ath. Pol.* 7.1). Thus, the tradition was probably based on oral reports or on inferences from the surviving homicide law. It is precisely this surviving law, however, that has led many scholars to reject the tradition of Drakon's severity.[16] Even if the preserved law applies only to unintentional homicide, it does not seem especially severe; and since it prescribes exile as a penalty, it seems to contradict Plutarch's statement quoted above.[17] Does this mean that the

---

to designate either death or exile as a penalty for homicide (*IG* I^2.10 [I^3.14] = *GHI* 40, lines 29–31). Though this is not strictly an Athenian law, it supports the conclusion we have reached about the Athenian penalties for homicide. Cf. Soph. *OT* 99–101.

14. See J. Miller, *RE* 5 (1905):1656 for other references.

15. Lyk. 65; Arist. *Pol.* 1274B16, *Rhet.* 1400B21; and Demades *apud* Plut. *Sol.* 17. The tradition may go back to Prodicus if we accept an emendation in Arist. *Rhet.* 1400B20; see Stroud, p. 66, n. 5.

16. See Miller (above, n. 14); Busolt-Swoboda, p. 815; and Ruschenbusch, "*phonos*," pp. 151–52.

17. Of course ἀνδροφόνοι in Plutarch's report might designate only intentional killers.

tradition of Drakon's severity must be rejected? Let us consider the problem from a different perspective.

If Drakon prescribed capital punishment for a large number of crimes, or even only for intentional homicide, by what authority and with what means could the state have executed those convicted of a capital crime? The strong central governments of the Near East or Egypt may have had facilities for imprisonment and execution of offenders, but it is hard to imagine that such facilities existed in the weak and decentralized Athenian polis of the seventh century. We do have evidence from a seventh-century (?) burial near Phaleron of the execution of seventeen people, apparently all at the same time, but these are likely to have been a group of public enemies, perhaps captured in battle.[18]

Moreover, it is unlikely that state control of the judicial process was by Drakon's time so developed that the state regularly carried out sentences of any sort in cases which were still essentially private suits, such as the δίκη φόνου. Whatever our view of the development of Greek legal procedure (see below, pp. 162–63), it is clear that in Drakon's time the plaintiff himself must have been primarily responsible for executing whatever settlement he may have been awarded by a court. Even in the fourth century a plaintiff who won a monetary settlement in a private suit had to execute the judgment himself and might have to seize by force what was owed him or else sue again (by a δίκη ἐξούλης) if the defendant did not pay.[19]

The preserved fragment of Drakon's law also contains

18. See Gernet, *REG* 37 (1924): 262–66, 278–79 (= *Anthropologie de la Grèce antique* [Paris, 1968], pp. 303–06, 317). He speculates that the victims were pirates, captured in war.

19. See Harrison, vol. 1, pp. 206–27; vol. 2, pp. 187–90. The δίκη ἐξούλης is at least as old as Solon (*SN* F36).

evidence of the importance of self-help in carrying out a
judicial sentence. The provision protecting an exiled killer
(lines 26–29) implies that individuals, not the state, will
see to it that the killer observes the proper terms of his
exile, and if our restoration of the next provision (lines
30ff.) is in general correct (see above, Chapter Three),
these lines make explicit the right of individuals to enforce
the sentence of exile. In other words, capital punishment
would not be enforced by the criminal's imprisonment and
execution by the state but rather by his death at the hands
of the injured party if he did not properly go into exile.

In addition, the clause allowing the killing of a plun-
derer or kidnapper caught in the act (lines 37–38)
specifically legitimizes self-help in this particular case, prohibiting vengeance by the assailant's family. This provision forms part of Drakon's homicide law, but we could
just as well describe it as a law prescribing the death penalty for a particular offense, seizure and kidnapping. Similarly, a law allowing the killing of an adulterer caught in
the act (which may have been part of Drakon's original
homicide law)[20] can easily be thought of as a prescription
of the death penalty for adultery rather than as a provision for lawful homicide. In fact the speaker in Lysias 1
cites this law (1.30) and then speaks (1.32) of the lawgiver "condemning them [adulterers] to death" (τῶν μὲν
θάνατον κατέγνω).[21]

---

20. Plutarch (*Sol.* 23.1) attributes the law on adultery to Solon.
A version of the law is preserved in Dem. 23.53; if it was part of
the homicide law, then Solon may have taken it over from Drakon.
Lysias (1.30) calls it a law of the Areopagos.

21. Ruschenbusch ("*phonos,*" pp. 149–51) includes wounding
and arson along with adultery and theft as crimes for which Drakon
wrote laws as part of his homicide law. There is no need to conclude, however, as he does (p. 151), that "Drakon in der Form des
Blutrechts ein ganzes Deliktsrecht gegeben hat." See Stroud, pp.
77–82.

Another feature of early legal procedure which is closely connected with the process of self-help is *atimia,* or outlawry.[22] In Drakon's time at least, to declare an offender *atimos* allowed anyone who wished within Attica to kill him with impunity,[23] and a declaration of *atimia* would thus have led inevitably to the offender's death or exile. This was the penalty for attempted tyranny in a law (*Ath. Pol.* 16.10) that probably goes back at least to Drakon,[24] and the procedure of declaring an offender *atimos* in this strong sense may have lasted until the fifth century, if Demosthenes' interpretation (9.44) of the decree against Arthmios of Zela is correct.[25] In any case, in Drakon's time a declaration of *atimia* was in effect a means of condemning someone to death unless he went into exile first.

Thus, it seems likely that in Drakon's time capital punishment carried out by the polis did not exist, except perhaps for special cases involving public enemies. Rather, the laws permitted instantaneous self-help in some cases (e.g., against an adulterer); for other offenses (e.g., homicide) a judicial verdict would allow the victim or his relatives to enforce the criminal's punishment; and the declaration of other offenders (e.g., would-be tyrants) as *atimoi* allowed anyone to kill them with impunity. In some cases more than one of these methods might apply.[26]

---

22. See Hansen, esp. pp. 75–82: "The corollary of outlawry is self-help and it is *per definitionem* incompatible with capital punishment enforced by the authorities" (p. 82).

23. Cf. Dem. 9.44: ἐν τοῖς φονικοῖς γέγραπται νόμοις, ὑπὲρ ὧν ἂν μὴ διδῷ φόνου δικάσασθαι, 'καὶ ἄτιμος' φησὶ 'τεθνάτω.'

24. Solon's amnesty decree (Plut. *Sol.* 19.4) shows that before his time some people (Kylon?) had been declared *atimoi* for attempted tyranny; see Ostwald, pp. 106–09.

25. See, e.g., Ruschenbusch, *Untersuchungen zur Geschichte des athenischen Strafrechts* (Cologne, 1968), p. 20, n. 58; Hansen, pp. 78–82; MacDowell, *CR,* n.s. 28 (1978):175.

26. Ais. 1.91 implies that a killer caught in the act could be

If this is an accurate picture, then Drakon probably did
not prescribe the death penalty as we understand it for
any offense. However, the allowance for self-help in many
of his laws was easily understood as a prescription of
death, which in effect it often was. When Lykourgos (1.65)
discusses the severity of the early lawgivers (and he probably has Drakon specifically in mind in this passage), he
says, "They did not set death as the penalty for the theft
of a hundred drachmas but a lesser penalty for the theft
of ten drachmas. Nor did they put to death the large-scale
temple robber but punish the small-scale robber with a
smaller penalty. Nor did they fine the killer of a slave but
ban ($\epsilon\tilde{\iota}\rho\gamma o\nu\ \tau\tilde{\omega}\nu\ \nu\acute{o}\mu\omega\nu$)[27] the killer of a freeman, but
they punished all crimes alike with death." The parallel
structure of these three sentences indicates that Lykourgos
understood the banishment of the killer of a citizen to be
equivalent to a death penalty. Thus, when the ancient writers speak of Drakon's having prescribed death for a large
number of offenses, they are probably referring not to laws
explicitly prescribing a trial and public execution for all
these offenders, but rather to other procedures that would
in fact lead to their death or (more often) exile.

In sum, it is very unlikely that Drakon explicitly prescribed death as a penalty for intentional homicide. Rather,
the primary penalty was exile, to which was probably
added a declaration of *atimia*. Death would result only if
the convicted killer did not obey the prescription of
exile. That at least some convicted killers were in exile a

---

executed by anyone on the spot, and Solon's amnesty decree (Plut.
Sol. 19.4) indicates that killers who were exiled were also declared
atimoi.

27. "This prohibition is identical with total *atimia,*" says Hansen (p. 70), though he takes the phrase here to refer to exile (p. 70,
n. 21).

generation after Drakon's law is indicated clearly by Solon's amnesty decree,[28] and we have no reason to doubt that exile was in fact the most common penalty for homicide in Drakon's time, just as it probably was both before him and in the fourth century.

If this is a correct analysis of the means by which a death penalty was effected in Drakon's time, we may accept the first sentence of Drakon's law as applying to both intentional and unintentional homicide, without contradicting ancient testimony that Drakon prescribed the death penalty for homicide as well as for many other crimes. He did this by prescribing exile as the penalty for homicide but allowing (probably in lines 30–31) the killer who was not in exile to be killed with impunity.

Exactly this procedure seems to be envisioned by Demosthenes in his explanation (23.38) of the provision of Drakon's law (lines 26–29) forbidding the killing of an exiled killer: ἐκεῖνος [sc. Drakon] ᾤετο τὸν πεφευγότ᾽ ἐπ᾽ αἰτίᾳ φόνου καὶ ἑαλωκότα, ἐάνπερ ἅπαξ ἐκφύγῃ καὶ σωθῇ, εἴργειν μὲν τῆς τοῦ παθόντος πατρίδος δίκαιον εἶναι, κτείνειν δ᾽ οὐχ ὅσιον ἀπανταχοῦ. ("Drakon thought that with regard to one who had stood trial[29] on a charge of homicide and had been convicted, once he should go safely into exile, it was right to bar him from the victim's fatherland but it was not righteous to kill him everywhere.") There is no reason to doubt that Demosthenes has in mind here cases of intentional (as well as unintentional)

---

28. Plut. *Sol.* 19.4; see below. It is impossible to understand φόνῳ in the amnesty decree as designating only unintentional homicide, and σφαγαῖσιν too must imply primarily, it not solely, intentional killing.

29. For φεύγειν as "stand trial" see above, n. 8. Here a compound verb (ἐκφύγῃ) is used to indicate exile, making this sense of φεύγειν even clearer by contrast.

homicide, and it is clear that he envisions in such cases a
process of trial, conviction, and then exile.[30] Moreover,
the last word implies that the convicted killer could be
killed in some places, presumably in Attica.

This conclusion is confirmed in another passage (20.
157–58), where Demosthenes discusses the special atten-
tion given by the law to homicides committed in vengeance (οἱ περὶ ἀλλήλους φόνοι):[31] "Now in the laws
concerning these offenses Drakon, though making it clear
that to kill another is a fearful and terrible thing, and
though banning the killer from holy water, libations, com-
munal mixing-bowls, sacrifices, and the agora, nonetheless
did not deprive him of judicial procedure, but laid down
conditions in which killing was allowed, and if someone
killed in such circumstances, he provided that he would not
be polluted." Demosthenes is here referring directly to
Drakon's homicide law[32] and is emphasizing (in the first
part of the sentence) the severity of Drakon's treatment

---

30. It is possible that this order of events (trial, conviction, and
then exile) was also common in Demosthenes' time, since some who
were convicted of intentional homicide and sentenced to death
may have fled before their execution and gone safely into exile,
where presumably they would be protected by the law. The con-
versation between Crito and Socrates (*Crito* 44C5–45C4) implies
that an escape into exile before execution was easily arranged
and was acceptable to many Athenians.

31. That these homicides περὶ ἀλλήλους are intentional homicides is implied by the expression itself and is confirmed by Demosthenes' mention of the Areopagos as the protector against such
offenses and his use of the term αὐτόχειρ; see Stroud, p. 38.

32. The list of places from which the killer is barred in Dem.
20.158 does not correspond to the places from which an exiled killer
is barred in Drakon's law, lines 27–28, since Demosthenes is probably referring to the initial proclamation barring the accused killer
from τῶν νομίμων.

of intentional homicide. It is hard to explain why he would
not mention the death penalty for intentional homicide
if Drakon had explicitly prescribed it.

There is no reason to think that the same conditions
did not hold in the case of unintentional homicide. Neither
Drakon's provision protecting the exiled killer (lines 26–
29) nor the later law (Dem. 23.28) allowing killers caught
in Attica to be killed with impunity makes any distinction between intentional and unintentional homicide (the
word in both cases is ἀνδροφόνος), and it seems unlikely
that such a distinction existed in Drakon's law.

Exile, though undoubtedly preferable to death for most
people, was a very severe penalty. Unless one had rich
and influential friends in other cities, exile generally meant
a wretched life of poverty, since even if one's property
was not confiscated it seems unlikely that one could take
anything of value into exile. This makes it all the more
likely that exile was considered a true penalty for homicide and not a means of avoiding a penalty. As the defendant in Antiphon's *First Tetralogy* puts it (Ant. 2.2.9),
"If I am convicted and put to death, I shall leave unholy
disgrace for my children, or going into exile, an old man
without a country, I shall be a beggar in a foreign land."[33]

We can conclude, then, that Drakon's law set the
primary penalty for homicide, whether intentional or unintentional, as exile. Once convicted by the Ephetai and
declared guilty by the kings, if the killer did not go into

---

33. There are some interesting remarks on the equivalence of
exile and death as punishments in Fustel de Coulanges, *La Cité
antique* (Paris, 1864), p. 236. Note also that the Chalkis decree (*IG*
I².39 [I³.40] = *GHI* 52, lines 71–74) provides that Chalkidians
cannot appeal their case to Athens "unless the penalty is exile, death,
or *atimia*" (πλὴν φυγῆς καὶ θανάτου καὶ ἀτιμίας), which suggests
that these penalties were all of the same degree of severity. Cf. *IG*
I².101 (I³.96), lines 7–8.

exile he could be killed with impunity. Differences between the conditions of exile for intentional and unintentional killers may have been specified, either in the original law or by later amendment (cf. Dem. 23.72), and after Drakon's time supplementary provisions to his law must have established a sharper delineation between the treatment of intentional and unintentional homicide. Along with the specification of a different court for intentional homicide (see below), a provision was probably added concerning the length of exile for intentional and unintentional homicide, and perhaps also a provision prescribing capital punishment for any convicted intentional killer who awaited a court verdict. Such a process would account for the fact that although Drakon's original homicide law was still in force in the fourth century, the penalty for someone convicted of intentional homicide who awaited the court's verdict changed from exile to "death and exile." The practical effect of such a change, however, was probably minor, since exile remained the common penalty for all homicide. As a scholion to *Iliad* 2.665 puts it, Ἑλληνικόν ἐστι τὸ μὴ φόνῳ φόνον λύειν, φυγαδεύειν δὲ τὸν ἅπαντα χρόνον.[34]

Finally, the tradition of the severity of Drakon's laws can be ascribed to his practice of allowing a lawful homicide in the case of certain specific offenses and declaring the offender *atimos* in other cases. In fact these provisions probably resulted in few deaths; many thieves, for example, even those caught in the act, must have been forced to return the property and pay an extra fine to the victim rather than be executed on the spot. But such provisions

---

34. The scholion continues, ὅθεν Σόλων ἔτη πέντε ὥρισεν (*SN* F7). It is hard to say whether five years was a maximum time, intended to reduce the period of exile for unintentional homicide, or a minimum time, intended to increase it for intentional homicide.

might appear to be a general prescription of the death penalty and could thus give rise to a tradition of much greater severity than actual conditions warranted. If this analysis is correct, even unintentional homicide could have been thought to be punished by death, though the treatment of unintentional homicide in the preserved law seems relatively lenient.

The second difficulty raised by our interpretation of Drakon's law concerns the homicide courts. We know that in the fourth century intentional homicide was tried before the Areopagos (Dem. 23.67, *Ath. Pol.* 57.3), and it is often assumed that the same was true in Drakon's time.[35] If, however, the preserved provisions of Drakon's law apply to intentional as well as unintentional homicide, then trials for intentional homicide in Drakon's time were conducted by the Ephetai and not by the Areopagos.[36] Although there has been much debate[37] about the relationship between the two bodies in this early period and about the composition and duties of each, no agreement has emerged and perhaps none is possible with the limited evidence we have. But even if no certain conclusion is possible about the composition of the Ephetai and their relation to the Areopagos, the evidence is for the most part consistent with our interpretation of Drakon's law. Those who subscribe to more traditional views of Drakon's law also find it difficult to account for some of this evidence, and some have argued that the Areopagos did not try cases of intentional homicide until Solon's time or later.[38]

---

35. See, e.g., Busolt-Swoboda, p. 811; Hignett, p. 80; Stroud, p. 36.

36. I am assuming for the moment that the Areopagos and the Ephetai were two separate bodies.

37. See above, n. 35, and for earlier views Busolt-Swoboda, p. 803, n. 4.

38. Among those who hold that Drakon's law on intentional

In the law itself the provision protecting the exiled killer (lines 26–29) provides that anyone killing him "will be liable to the same treatment as one who kills an Athenian, and the Ephetai shall decide." This provision must include the intentional killing of an exiled killer (see above, Chapter Three), and since these killers are to be judged by the Ephetai, it is implied that those who intentionally kill an Athenian are also to be tried by this body[39] and not by the Areopagos. Other evidence, however, seems to suggest that the Areopagos always tried intentional homicide, and we must discuss the history of this court before turning to the question of the identity and function of the Ephetai.

The only early evidence to support the view that the Areopagos was a pre-Solonian homicide court is the ascription of a number of mythical homicide trials to this court. Hellanikos (*FGH* 323a F22; cf. F1) lists four early defendants at the Areopagos: Orestes, Ares, Kephalos, and Daidalos. Jacoby notes that these trials include intentional, unintentional, and lawful homicide[40] and accepts the implication that in its earliest period (before Drakon) the Areopagos tried all cases of homicide. But there are difficulties with this view. The earliest extant version of a

---

homicide was later revised (and removed from his first axon), many (e.g., Ruschenbusch, "*phonos,*" pp. 130–31) believe that the assignment of jurisdiction over intentional homicide to the Areopagos was one reason for this revision.

39. ἐν τοῖς αὐτοῖς ἐνέχεσθαι implies that the trial takes place in the same court; see above, chap. 3, n. 30.

40. *FGH*, vol. 3B, Supplements I.22–25 and II.19–29. In fact Orestes' killing of Klytaimestra is not an example of lawful homicide according to Athenian law as we know it (unless we were to argue tyrannicide). On the other hand, Ares' killing of Halirrothios, who was trying to rape Ares' daughter, is a true example of lawful homicide.

homicide trial before the Areopagos is Orestes' trial in Aischylos's *Eumenides,* and Jacoby accepts the common opinion that this trial was an Aischylean invention. He maintains,[41] however, that the legends of the other three trials probably go back to the pre-Drakontian period, when (in his view) the Areopagos judged all homicide. In my view there is no reason why these other legends could not have been created in the sixth or fifth centuries as aetiological myths similar to those concerning the other homicide courts, which Jacoby accepts as post-Drakontian.[42] The historical accuracy of such myths is certainly doubtful, and Hellanikos's testimony is thus of little significance.

The legend of the trial of Orestes before the Areopagos also appears in a slightly different form—trial by the twelve gods sitting as the court of the Areopagos—in Demosthenes 23.66, where he adds, "These are old matters, but as for more recent times, this is the only court from which neither tyrant nor oligarchy nor democracy has dared to remove homicide trials." Demosthenes' account is belied by the fact that he states elsewhere his belief that cases of lawful homicide, such as Orestes', were in his day tried at the Delphinion (23.74), but even if true, his remarks in 23.66 would prove only that once the Areopagos was assigned homicide cases, it continued to be a homicide court. Demosthenes may well be thinking of the reforms of Ephialtes, which apparently gave most of the functions of the Areopagos, except its jurisdiction in homicide cases, to other bodies.[43]

In sum, the legends concerning early homicide trials at the Areopagos and other statements of the court's antiquity[44] attest the respect it was accorded in the fifth century

---

41. Ibid., II.22, n. 22.
42. Ibid., n. 19.
43. See Arist. *Ath. Pol.* 25.2, Philochoros *FGH* 328 F64.
44. See Lys. 1.30, where the speaker refers to the ancestral

and later but not necessarily any historical situation, and
are thus of little help in establishing whether or not the
Areopagos was in fact a homicide court in the seventh century.

On the other hand, there is no positive evidence from
this period against the view that the Areopagos was originally a homicide court, though the testimony of the *Athe-
naion Politeia* may provide an argument *ex silentio*. On
three occasions in his discussion of early Athenian institutions Aristotle describes the powers of the Areopagos—
before Drakon's time (3.6), in Drakon's (putative) legislation (4.4), and in Solon's legislation (8.4)—but nowhere
does he mention the body's jurisdiction over homicide
cases.[45] The argument *ex silentio* is not a strong one,[46]
but it suggests that Aristotle found no historical support
for the mythical tradition of early homicide trials at
the Areopagos.

Compared with this inconclusive evidence, Plutarch's
remarks in *Solon* 19 seem to provide a firmer basis for
discussion.[47] After stating the view that Solon established
the Areopagos, Plutarch adds that most writers take this
view, which seems to have strong support from the fact
that "Drakon nowhere names the Areopagos, but in homicide matters (περὶ τῶν φονικῶν) always speaks of the
Ephetai." On the other side of the question, however, Plutarch cites a law of Solon: ἀτίμων ὅσοι ἄτιμοι ἦσαν πρὶν

---

tradition (πάτριόν ἐστι) that homicide cases were judged by the
Areopagos.

45. It is possible that τοὺς ἀκοσμοῦντας in *Ath. Pol.* 3.6 includes
killers, but the expression seems rather to indicate public offenders
(cf. Dem. 24.92).

46. See J. Miller, *RE* 5 (1905):1652.

47. Plutarch's source for *Solon* 19 was probably Didymos; see
Jacoby, *FGH*, vol. 3B, Supplements I.115 and II.110, n. 40.

ἢ Σόλωνα ἄρξαι, ἐπιτίμους εἶναι, πλὴν ὅσοι ἐξ 'Αρείου
πάγου ἢ ὅσοι ἐκ τῶν ἐφετῶν ἢ ἐκ πρυτανείου καταδικασθέντες ὑπὸ τῶν βασιλέων ἐπὶ φόνῳ ἢ σφαγαῖσιν ἢ ἐπὶ
τυραννίδι ἔφευγον ὅτε ὁ θεσμὸς ἐφάνη ὅδε—"Of present
outlaws, those who were outlawed before Solon took
office shall be restored to their full rights, except those
who, having been pronounced guilty by the kings[48] on
a charge of homicide or slaughter[49] or tyranny, were in
exile from the Areopagos or from the Ephetai or from
the Prytaneion when this law was announced." Plutarch
observes that this amnesty decree proves that the Areopagos must have existed before Solon, and after some discussion of possible ambiguity in the decree he leaves the
question open.

We are thus presented with two strong but apparently
conflicting pieces of evidence: first, that there was no
mention of the Areopagos in Drakon's homicide law (probably the only law of Drakon available to Plutarch's sources),
and second, that a law of Solon mentions those previously
exiled from the Areopagos. The amnesty decree is almost
certainly Solonian,[50] and the testimony of Plutarch's sources
as to the absence of the Areopagos from Drakon's law is

48. I take the basileis here to be the same as in Drakon's law
(line 12); indeed, the mention of the Prytaneion here may support
the view that these are the basileus and the four phylobasileis. The
verb καταδικασθέντες presumably refers to the same activity as
δικάζειν in Drakon's law (lines 12–13); see above, chap. 3.

49. The term σφαγαί probably ‹designates political massacres (as
distinct from ordinary homicide, φόνος); in classical times, at least,
the term is generally applied to killing during political turmoil (see,
e.g., Xen. Hel. 2.2.6, 4.4.2; Isok. 5.107, 8.96). In Solon's amnesty
decree the term may refer specifically to the killing of the Kylonians;
see Hignett, p. 313, and for other views A. Ledl, Studien zur älteren
athenischen Verfassungsgeschichte (Heidelberg, 1914), p. 310.

50. The decree is cited as the eighth law on the thirteenth axon,

hard to dispute. The law was publicly recorded (on our stele
and perhaps also on the surviving original axones), and
scholars on the other side of the dispute would presumably
have had no trouble finding mention of the Areopagos if
there was one. How are we to explain this apparent conflict? The answer is simple: we accept the evidence of both
sides and conclude that the Areopagos existed before Solon
(cf. Ar. *Pol.* 1274A1–2), but not as a homicide court.

The only difficulty with this solution is that modern
scholars (unlike Plutarch)[51] have traditionally interpreted
the amnesty decree to mean not only that the Areopagos
existed before Solon but also that it was a homicide court.
Apparently their sole reason (aside from preconceptions
about the nature of the early Areopagos) is that the apparent balance of the phrasing of the decree (ἐξ 'Αρείου πάγου
. . . τῶν ἐφετῶν . . . πρυτανείου . . . ἐπὶ φόνῳ . . . σφαγαῖσιν
. . . τυραννίδι) may imply a relation between the Areopagos
and homicide. Ruschenbusch has recently disputed this
conclusion,[52] and even if one does not accept his argument
that the alignment of phrases must be chiastic (ἐξ 'Αρείου
πάγου with ἐπὶ τυραννίδι and ἐκ τῶν ἐφετῶν ἢ ἐκ πρυτανείου with ἐπὶ φόνῳ ἢ σφαγαῖσιν),[53] one must admit that
there is no necessity for the three courts and the three

---

and almost all critics accept it as genuine. The objections of Hignett
are answered by Ruschenbusch, *SN,* p. 7.

51. Plutarch notes that the amnesty decree implies that Solon
was not the first to give the Areopagos the power to judge cases
(τὸ κρίνειν), but he does not specify homicide cases.

52. "*Phonos,*" pp. 132–35. Ruschenbusch is not the only one to
suggest that the three terms in each series need not correspond in
order; see, e.g., Hignett, p. 312 and T. Lenschau, *RE* 7A.2 (1939):
1805–06, with references to earlier literature.

53. I shall have more to say about chiasmus in early prose in
Chapter Eight.

charges to correspond precisely in the order in which they are listed.

In fact Ruschenbusch's conclusions correspond well with what we know of the courts in Drakon's time and should be accepted for this reason. The Ephetai certainly judged some cases of homicide (φόνος) in Drakon's time, no matter how one interprets his homicide law. And if we ask where cases of attempted tyranny were tried before Solon, we shall most likely conclude that they were tried at the Areopagos,[54] which was apparently from its inception charged with overseeing the highest matters of state and public order[55] (see *Ath. Pol.* 3.6, 4.4, 8.4).[56] Since it is thus likely that the Areopagos judged cases of treason and that the Ephetai judged at least some cases of homicide,[57] there is no reason to interpret Solon's amnesty

---

54. See Ostwald, pp. 103–14.

55. We tend to consider homicide as serious a crime as treason, but this was not true for the Greeks. See G. Calhoun, *The Growth of Criminal Law in Ancient Greece* (Berkeley, 1927), pp. 8–11, on the excessive concern of modern scholars with homicide law as an essential part of criminal law. Most primitive people make treason a crime earlier than they do homicide; see Diamond, p. 62.

56. According to Aristotle (*Ath. Pol.* 8.4) Solon instituted a new law establishing the procedure of *eisangelia*, under which the Areopagos judged cases of "subversion of the democracy" (κατάλυσις τοῦ δήμου); we do not know if this law established a new procedure or allowed an existing one to be used in a new case.

57. The mention of the Prytaneion here is puzzling. We know (Dem. 23.76) that in the fourth century the Prytaneion tried cases in which the killer was unknown or in which only an animal or an inanimate object was held responsible. If the court had these same duties in Drakon's time, then it would not have exiled any specific killers; perhaps, as Hignett (p. 312) suggests, the inclusion of this court was necessary in order to exclude from the amnesty previous killers who had not yet been discovered.

decree as evidence that the Areopagos was a pre-Solonian
homicide court. Plutarch rightly concludes that the
Areopagos existed before Solon, and his evidence supports
the conclusion that the Areopagos was not a homicide
court in Drakon's time. Thus, we may abide by our view
that both intentional and unintentional homicide were
tried by the Ephetai under the provisions of Drakon's law.
This brings us, however, to our next difficulty: who were
the Ephetai?

The Ephetai (or "the fifty-one, the Ephetai" or "the
fifty-one") are mentioned six times in the preserved fragment of Drakon's law. [58] They judge cases of homicide
or planning a homicide (line 13); they judge unintentional
homicide (17); they appoint phratry members for the
purpose of pardoning an unintentional killer when no relatives survive (19); they judge cases of killing or being
responsible for the death of an exiled killer (29); and they
are involved in at least two other matters, perhaps the
killing of an accused killer before his trial (24–25) and homicide cases in which the plea is self-defense (35–36).
Except for the basileis, who apparently certify the verdict,
they are the only officials named in the preserved part
of the inscription, and it thus appears that they decided
all cases of homicide and matters directly relating to
homicide. [59]

The exceptions may have been the special cases of
homicide by an unknown killer or an animal or an inani-

---

58. I cannot account for this variation in the designation of the
Ephetai; see Stroud, pp. 48–49, who rejects one attempt to find
significance in the variation.

59. Cf. Pollux 8.125: ἐφέται . . . ἐδίκαζον δὲ τοῖς ἐφ' αἵματι
διωκομένοις ἐν τοῖς πέντε δικαστηρίοις. Σόλων δ' αὐτοῖς προσκατέ-
στησε τὴν ἐξ 'Αρείου πάγου βουλήν; and Harpokration s.v. ἐφέται:
οἱ δικάζοντες τὰς ἐφ' αἵματι κρίσεις ἐπὶ Παλλαδίῳ καὶ ἐπὶ Πρυτανείῳ
καὶ ἐπὶ Δελφινίῳ καὶ ἐν Φρεατοῖ ἐφέται ἐκαλοῦντο.

mate object, which were probably tried at the Prytaneion (see above, n. 57). The evidence as to whether the Ephetai were members of this court is conflicting but seems to me to indicate that they were not. Solon's amnesty decree mentions the Prytaneion as a body separate from the Ephetai, and Aristotle seems to ignore the Prytaneion when discussing the jurors in homicide courts in the *Politics* (1300B24–30); furthermore, in an apparent reference to the Prytaneion in *Ath. Pol.* 57.4,[60] Aristotle speaks only of judgment by the basileus and the phylobasileis. From this evidence MacDowell (p. 88) suggests that Harpokration and Pollux (see above, n. 59) or their source(s) were mistaken in stating that the Ephetai tried cases at the Prytaneion.

MacDowell's view is plausible, especially in view of the nature of the cases tried at this court. If the court's duty was simply to convict nonhuman killers or to pronounce a verdict against unknown killers, then only rarely, if ever, would a case before this court be disputed,[61] and there would thus have been no need for jurors to serve here in addition to the basileus and the phylobasileis. In Drakon's time, then, the Ephetai most likely tried only those homicide cases involving a known human defendant.

In the fourth century the role of the Ephetai was, as far as we can tell, the same as in Drakon's time, except that trials for intentional homicide were now under the jurisdiction of the Areopagos. The other kinds of homicide were judged by the Ephetai sitting at the Palladion, at the Delphinion, and in Phreatto.[62] Their authority must

---

60. See MacDowell, p. 86.

61. See Wolff, p. 78.

62. MacDowell (pp. 52–56) rejects the view that the duties of the Ephetai may have been taken over by ordinary dicasts in the fourth century; cf. Harrison, vol. 2, pp. 40–41.

have continued to be derived from Drakon's homicide law (see the quotations from this law in Dem. 23.37–38, 43.57), and to our knowledge they had no duties other than those connected with homicide cases.

MacDowell (pp. 51–52) and others have suggested that the Ephetai may have been members of the Areopagos, but the evidence on this point is generally considered inconclusive.[63] On the one hand, Solon's amnesty decree and Patrokleides' decree modeled on it (And. 1.78) mention the Areopagos and the Ephetai separately, which seems to indicate that they were considered separate bodies. On the other hand, Demosthenes quotes the law providing protection for an exiled killer (23.37 = Drakon's law, lines 26–29) in the context of the laws of the Areopagos concerning intentional homicide. As we have seen (above, Chapter Three), this law indicates that the intentional killing of an exiled killer will be judged by the Ephetai (διαγιγνώσκειν δὲ τοὺς ἐφέτας), but it is almost certain that the intentional killing of an exiled killer, like the killing of an Athenian, would be judged by the Areopagos. Thus, this law seems to imply that the Ephetai were in fact members of the Areopagos.

One could perhaps answer the objection based on the two amnesty decrees by assuming that the Ephetai were a "committee" of the Areopagos but were considered a separate entity from the whole body, but then one would have to explain why the law in Dem. 23.37 apparently uses the name *Ephetai* to designate the whole Areopagos. The dilemma, that the Areopagos and the Ephetai seem

---

63. There is no explicit statement in our sources that the Ephetai were members of the Areopagos. The fact that Pollux (above, n. 59) says the Ephetai judged homicide cases at "the five courts" seems to imply that they belonged to the Areopagos, but his next statement seems to deny this implication, and thus his evidence is of no use.

at times to be referred to as one and the same body but at other times as two separate bodies, remains.

I think this dilemma can best be resolved by the following hypothesis, which is based on my understanding of the historical development of the homicide laws. Originally the Ephetai, a special body of fifty-one jurors, judged all homicide cases. They were a body separate from the Areopagos and thus are mentioned separately from them in the two amnesty decrees. They are also the only jurors mentioned by Drakon in his homicide law. Later an amendment to this law gave the council of the Areopagos jurisdiction in cases of intentional homicide, but the Ephetai retained their jurisdiction over other kinds of homicide. The wording of the original provisions of Drakon's law, however, remained unchanged, and the term *the Ephetai,* which had come to be more or less equivalent to "homicide jurors," was thereafter understood to refer either to the body of fifty-one who judged cases of homicide in the three other homicide courts, or to the Areopagos sitting as a homicide court (and perhaps even to the phylobasileis sitting as a homicide court at the Prytaneion). In common speech the name *Ephetai* indicated a body separate from the Areopagos and one would not use the term in a new law to refer to this court, but when found in the old laws in reference to a function now filled by the Areopagos, the name would designate that court.[64]

---

64. I have not used the evidence of *Ath. Pol.* 57.4 concerning the jurors in homicide cases because of the textual problem caused by a lacuna in the papyrus at a crucial point. Kenyon's restoration [ἐφέται] is now doubted, and ἄν[δ]ρ[ε]ς seems to be the correct reading (see Mortimer Chambers, *TAPA* 96 [1965]:38–39). Stroud (*CP* 63 [1968]:212) has conjectured that we should read δικάζουσι δ' οἱ λαχόντες ταῦτα ⟨να'⟩ ἄνδρες, πλὴν τῶν ἐν Ἀρείῳ πάγῳ γιγνομένων. If this conjecture is correct, the fact that Aristotle does not use the name *Ephetai* may suggest that it could in

We may conclude from this discussion that the problem of the early Areopagos and its relation to the Ephetai presents no serious obstacle to our interpretation of the first sentence of Drakon's homicide law, and we may thus accept the implication of this interpretation, that in Drakon's time the Ephetai judged all cases of homicide except perhaps at the Prytaneion. At some later date (or dates) jurisdiction over the different kinds of homicide was distributed among different courts, in three of which the Ephetai continued to act as jurors. The exception was the Areopagos, which already existed as an important council and which was put in charge of cases of intentional homicide. The law that effected this change must have been an amendment to Drakon's law, though kept separate from it;[65] perhaps it was inscribed only on the stele from the Areopagos (see above, pp. 26–28). It may in fact be the law preserved in Dem. 23.22: δικάζειν δὲ τὴν βουλὴν τὴν ἐν Ἀρείῳ πάγῳ φόνου καὶ τραύματος ἐκ προνοίας καὶ πυρκαιᾶς καὶ φαρμάκων, ἐάν τις ἀποκτείνῃ δούς—"The Council of the Areopagos will judge cases of homicide and wounding with intent [to kill] and arson and poisoning, if one kills by giving it."

The precise date of this amendment is uncertain. It has

certain contexts be understood to refer to the Areopagites and that Aristotle avoids it here because of this ambiguity. But this is mere speculation. Cf. also Aristotle's summary in the *Politics* (1300B25) of the different kinds of homicide courts, "whether they consist of the same jurors or others" (ἄν τ' ἐν τοῖς αὐτοῖς δικασταῖς ἄν τ' ἐν ἄλλοις), which seems to mean that the same jurors (i.e., the Ephetai) sit in some courts but not in others (i.e., the Areopagos).

65. The law transferring jurisdiction to the Areopagos must have been somehow separated from the original text of Drakon's law, or else Plutarch's sources in *Sol.* 19 would have found the name of the Areopagos in Drakon's homicide law.

been maintained[66] that the use of δικάζειν to mean "judge" (cf. δικάζειν = "pronounce a verdict" in Drakon's law, lines 11–12) indicates that the amendment is later than Solon, but the scarcity of evidence for the use of this verb in the sixth century renders this argument inconclusive.[67] Certainly the transferral of cases must have taken place before Ephialtes' reforms in 462, since these left the Areopagos in charge of homicide cases.[68] Moreover, Aristotle's story (*Ath. Pol.* 16.8)[69] that Peisistratos was once hailed before the Areopagos on a charge of homicide, if true, implies that Solon was the author of this change.

Whatever the date of this change in jurisdiction, a new stele was inscribed at the same time or later with the homicide laws pertaining to the Areopagos (see above, Chapter Two), from which Demosthenes quotes (23.22). This new stele contained excerpts from Drakon's law, in some of which (Dem. 23.37) the term *Ephetai* occurred. Although this term did not traditionally apply to the Areopagos, it was left unchanged and was easily understood to refer to the Areopagos as a body of "homicide jurors."

One more discrepancy between Drakon's law as we have interpreted it and fourth-century practice remains to

---

66. Ruschenbusch, "*phonos,*" pp. 131–32, with further references p. 132, n. 14.

67. For δικάζειν in Drakon's law (lines 11–12), see above, chap. 3. Note also that in Dem. 23.22 δικάζειν is followed by a genitive of the charge, whereas in Drakon's law it is probably followed by an accusative (and infinitive?); this may account for the difference in meaning. Aly (p. 11, n. 17) sees the use of ἀποκτείνειν in Dem. 23.22 as evidence of its being later than Drakon, since the compound verb does not appear in the preserved fragment; but cf. above, chap. 3, n. 85.

68. See Philochoros *FGH* 328 F64.

69. Cf. *Pol.* 1315B21–22 and Plut. *Sol.* 31.3.

be considered, the question of pardon in cases of intentional homicide. It seems very probable that in the fourth century exile for intentional homicide was permanent (ἀειφυγίᾳ, Dem. 21.43) and that pardon was not allowed. This is indicated by Demosthenes' statement (23.77) that the special court in Phreatto, which tried exiled killers accused of another homicide, was available to those convicted of unintentional homicide; he appears to exclude intentional killers from this procedure, presumably because these could never be readmitted to Attica even if acquitted of the second charge of homicide. Furthermore, the speaker in Dem. 37.58–59 (= 38.21–22) discusses the granting of pardon in cases of unintentional homicide in order to argue that if reconciliation is possible in the case of such a serious crime, it is undoubtedly legitimate in his own, less serious case. Surely the speaker would have mentioned the possibility of pardon for intentional homicide if it existed.

It was possible, however, for the victim before he died to pardon the intentional killer, as we learn from the same passage (37.59).[70] It also seems to have been possible, in cases of intentional homicide, for the relatives of the victim to reach a monetary settlement with the killer and refrain from prosecuting. The speaker in Dem. 58.28–29 denounces such an arrangement,[71] but he does not call it illegal even though in the same passage (58.29) he criticizes

---

70. That the possibility of pardon by the victim himself exists in cases of intentional as well as unintentional homicide is clear from the speaker's reference to the penalties the killer would otherwise suffer, namely, "banishment, exile, and death" (Dem. 37.59). See also Eur. *Hipp.* 1449; cf. above, chap. 3, n.5.

71. It is not certain in this case just what kind of homicide was committed. The speaker uses the rather vague expression βιαίῳ θανάτῳ (58.28), which probably indicates both intentional and unintentional homicide but not lawful homicide (see below). Of course if the relatives do not choose to prosecute, there would never

the illegality of another activity of the victim's relative. Surely he would have labeled the agreement not to prosecute illegal if it had been so.[72] It seems, then, that there was no legal obligation for a relative to prosecute, though there may well have been a strong social and moral obligation.[73]

In Drakon's law pardon apparently was possible for intentional homicide unless none of the victim's relatives survived (lines 13–19, see above, Chapter Three). Monetary arrangements before the trial and exile were also possible under both Drakon[74] and Solon.[75] Thus, the change in the provision for pardon between Drakon and the fourth century was probably concerned only with the terms of exile for the intentional killer, and a relatively simple amendment stating that exile for intentional

---

be a legal determination of the nature of the homicide, and the speaker may therefore be speaking with deliberate vagueness.

72. MacDowell (pp. 8–9) speaks of a bribe in this case, but the Greek (ἀργύριον λαβών) does not warrant the conclusion that the activity was illegal. Nor does Harpokration's description of ὑποφόνια (s.v.) as money paid to the victim's relatives ἵνα μὴ ἐπεξίωσιν imply anything illegal about the arrangement, as MacDowell claims. A similar description could be used of out-of-court settlements in modern civil suits, which are perfectly legal.

73. In Antiphon 1 the speaker criticizes his half-brothers for not having prosecuted their mother after their father's death (and for defending her now), but he mentions no legal obligation to do so, and evidently a rather long time has passed during which they apparently suffered nothing for not having prosecuted.

74. Pollux (9.61 = SN F10) says it was possible under Drakon's law to pay twenty cattle in compensation (κἂν τοῖς Δράκοντος νόμοις ἔστιν ἀποτίνειν εἰκοσάβοιον); the reference is probably to the homicide law.

75. SN F11, F12. The fact that Solon apparently discussed such payments in his own laws may indicate he was revising or refining regulations already existing in Drakon's laws.

homicide would be perpetual could have accomplished this change.[76]

Thus, it appears that the differences between the treatment of intentional homicide in fourth-century Athenian law as we know it and in Drakon's law, though not insignificant, are not so great as is sometimes thought and could easily have come about by a process of amendment. The three changes I have discussed—the designation of death as the penalty for intentional homicide, the transfer of cases of intentional homicide to the jurisdiction of the Areopagos, and the prohibition of pardon after conviction for intentional homicide—all provide a greater differentiation between intentional and unintentional homicide. There is no doubt that in the fourth century this distinction was important in Athenian homicide law, though it was not so great as in our law, in which unintentional homicide is not punished at all.

In Drakon's law, although intentional homicide was distinguished from unintentional, the basic treatment of the two was the same; only in relatively minor details did they differ. This situation may be difficult to accept without a few additional considerations.

In a number of other procedures in Athenian homicide cases intent seems to have been of little or no concern. All prosecutions for the killing of a noncitizen (metic, foreigner, or slave), for instance, were brought before the court of the Palladion (*Ath. Pol.* 57.3), and neither in Aristotle nor in any case described by the orators (e.g., Dem. 47.52–73,

---

76. Cf. Ruschenbusch, "*phonos,*" p. 138. There may also have been a change in the terms of exile for the unintentional killer (see above, n. 34), if it is true that in the fourth century there was some time limit for exile in these cases; MacDowell (pp. 122–23) doubts the existence of a time limit.

Isok. 18.52) is the factor of intent accorded significance.[77] Similarly, Demosthenes' description of the procedure of *apagoge* (23.80), in which a killer (ἀνδροφόνος) caught in certain public places could be arrested by anyone, makes no mention of intent.[78] An exception to the general lack of concern with intent in homicide laws may be indicated by the addition of the phrase βιαίῳ θανάτῳ to a number of Athenian proxeny decrees. These decrees often provide protection for a non-Athenian by stipulating that if anyone kills him, the death is to be treated just like the death of an Athenian. It appears that ca. 430 the regular expression ἐάν τις ἀπο-κτείνῃ is replaced by the formula ἐάν τις βιαίῳ θανάτῳ ἀποθάνῃ or ἐάν τις ἀποκτείνῃ βιαίῳ θανάτῳ.[79] It is not immediately clear precisely what sort of homicide the

---

77. The killing of the old woman in Dem. 47.52–73 is a case of intentional homicide, but the speaker does not specifically point this out. His concern is to make clear the close association between the woman and himself and the fact that her death was connected with his own house and property (cf. 47.68). The intentional nature of the killing per se is apparently of no interest to him.

78. Hansen, p. 101: "It is apparent from Demosthenes' description that an ἀπαγωγὴ φόνου could be employed against all types of homicide."

79. H. B. Mattingly (*Epigraphica* 36 [1974]:42–43) puts the date between 430 and 425, but the dates in Michael B. Walbank, *Athenian Proxenies of the Fifth Century B.C.* (Toronto, 1978), are slightly earlier. Following Walbank's texts and restorations we find three early (ca. 460–440) decrees with the simple ἀποκτείνῃ (*IG* I².27a, 28a, 56 [I³.27, 19, 156]) and ten later decrees (431/30–405/4) with the qualification βιαίῳ θανάτῳ (*IG* I².72, 143b, 144, 154; II².32, 38, 73; *SEG* X.50, 120? [*IG* I³.162, 28, 91, 164, 228, 161, 179, 57, 225] and *IG* II².8). Although a few of these texts are largely restored, the consistency of the evidence is striking.

phrase βιαίῳ θανάτῳ designates. In its literal sense ("a
violent death") it ought to include all cases of homicide,
intentional, unintentional, and lawful,[80] but many
scholars[81] assume that it designates only the first of these.
There is some evidence, however, that the phrase may
designate unlawful (that is, both intentional and unintentional) as opposed to lawful homicide.

The law concerning ἀνδροληψιον[82] quoted by Demosthenes (23.82) begins ἐάν τις βιαίῳ θανάτῳ ἀποθάνῃ, and
in his discussion of the law Demosthenes (23.83) glosses
βιαίῳ with ἀδίκως. This implies that the phrase here designates intentional and unintentional homicide together, as
opposed to lawful homicide. This interpretation of βιαίῳ
θανάτῳ gains some support from the fact that βίαιος is
equated with ἄνομος in Xenophon[83] and is glossed with
παράνομος by Hesychios.[84] Still, the evidence is not sufficient for certainty, and it is possible that the qualification βιαίῳ θανάτῳ designates intentional homicide and
that ἀδίκως is here used loosely to indicate intentional
homicide.[85]

---

80. The adjective βίαιος several times in Plato's *Laws* (865D7,
874D4, D6) designates any violent death, but Plato never uses the
phrase βιαίῳ θανάτῳ, which may have developed a narrower legal
sense than the simple adjective.

81. E.g., Mattingly (above, n. 79), p. 42.

82. The evidence is probably not sufficient for us to determine
exactly what procedures were followed in a case of ἀνδροληψιον; see
MacDowell, pp. 27–31. Neither of the descriptions of the procedure
in the later compilers mentions intent (see MacDowell, p. 28).

83. Xen. *Cyr.* 1.3.17: τὸ μὲν νόμιμον, δίκαιον· τὸ δὲ ἄνομον,
βίαιον.

84. Hesych. s.v. βίαιος. Cf. also the use of βιαίῳ θανάτῳ in Dem.
58.28 (see above, n. 71).

85. ἀδίκως is occasionally used as an equivalent to intentional, as
distinct from unintentional, homicide (Ant. 3.2.9, Ais. 2.88); see

Some have ascribed the law concerning ἀνδροληψιον to Drakon,[86] but the fact that βιαίῳ θανάτῳ is not found in inscriptions before about 430 suggests it is later than Drakon,[87] and the law seems to fit well with the "imperial" tone of the late-fifth-century proxeny decrees. Thus, whether the phrase designates only intentional homicide or (more likely) both intentional and unintentional homicide, this qualification was probably not introduced into Athenian law until long after Drakon.

Finally, there are several references to homicide in cities other than Athens, none of which suggests any difference between the treatment of intentional and unintentional homicide.[88] An Athenian decree containing regulations for Erythrai (*IG* I². 10 [I³.14] = *GHI* 40, lines 29–31)[89] includes a homicide law providing death or exile if one Erythraian kills another. A Cyrenaean inscription of the early fourth century (*SEG* 9.72 [= *GD* 115], sec. 19) describes various ritual practices necessary for the purification of a suppliant killer.[90] And an early Cumean

---

Gagarin, *GRBS* 19 (1978):291–306. At other times, however, it can designate "lawless" homicide; cf. ἐκὼν ἀδίκως in Dem. 23.50, where each term seems to have its full force, and βίᾳ ἀδίκως in Dem. 23.60 (cf. above, chap. 3, n. 92).

86. Ruschenbusch (*SN* F13), for example, includes it as one of Solon's, and therefore Drakon's, homicide laws. Demosthenes (23.86) simply says it comes from the homicide laws.

87. The earliest author cited by LSJ s.v. βίαιος is Herodotos.

88. Kurt Latte (*Hermes* 66 [1931]:133, n. 35 = *Kleine Schriften*, pp. 271–72, n. 35) lists several other Greek laws that he feels make or imply a distinction between intentional and unintentional actions. None of these is a homicide law, and in none is the distinction quite the same as that between intentional and unintentional homicide.

89. Meiggs-Lewis date the decree (*GHI* 40) to (?) 453/2.

90. The section begins ἱκέσιος τρίτος, αὐτοφόνος. There is no

law on homicide (περὶ τὰ φονικά), according to Aristotle
(*Pol.* 1269A1–3), provides for conviction if a certain number of witnesses are produced. In none of these cases is
there any indication that intent was a factor.[91] It may be
that all these laws and decrees were intended to apply
primarily to intentional homicide, but none of them ex-
cludes the possibility that they can be applied to unintentional homicide as well. The lawgivers apparently felt
no need to mention intent.

Of course the evidence from other cities and from
other procedures in Athens itself proves nothing about
Drakon's law. It does indicate, however, that the dichot-
omy between intentional and unintentional homicide
was not so important for the Greeks, even in the fourth
century, as it is for us, and this may make it easier to
accept the implication of my interpretation of Drakon's
law, namely, that the provisions concerning homicide
apply equally (with minor exceptions) to both intentional
and unintentional homicide.

---

indication what kind of homicide is implied by αὐτοφόνος. Obviously
it cannot imply suicide; most likely it simply means "killer." Cf.
Herod. 1.35.1–3, in which Kroisos purifies Adrastos before asking
about the homicide he has committed.

91. See Latte's discussion of these and other cases in *RE* 16.1
(1933): 278–81 (= *Kleine Schriften,* pp. 380–84). He concludes (pp. 280–81): "Überall in den angeführten Beispielen [mostly
inscriptions] ist Mord ein einheitlicher Begriff, der vom Ergebnis
her bestimmt wird; wer einen Mann erschlägt, ist Mörder, ohne dass
seine Absicht oder die sonstigen Umstände der Tat etwas daran
ändern (*Il.* 23.85, Hes. Frg. 144 Rz. [= 257 M–W]); es herrscht reine
Erfolgshaftung. Anscheinend hat sich dieser Zustand in vielen
griechischen Staaten ziemlich lange erhalten."

DRAKON'S HOMICIDE LAW: ORGANIZATION, STYLE, AND GENERAL PRINCIPLES

I should like to conclude this study with additional observations about the organization, style, and general nature of Drakon's homicide law in the context of the history of Athenian law and legal procedure. In order to facilitate these observations I present the law in as complete a form as possible and as a prose text rather than as an epigraphical document, using modern conventions of spelling, punctuation, and paragraphing, and omitting epigraphical notation.[1]

I have already observed that Drakon's homicide law is clearly and effectively organized. A more detailed consideration of the organization and purpose of the law reinforces this conclusion.[2] For convenience the separate provisions can be grouped in three major sections, lines 11–20, 20–33, and 33–38, which we shall consider in turn.[3]

---

1. In referring to the text I shall continue to use the line numbers of the inscription.

2. Aly (pp. 8–29) discusses the organization of what he considers to be Drakon's law, which is an amalgamation of provisions found on our stele and in Demosthenes. On the basis of the fifteen provisions that form his text he concludes that the organization is loose and rambling, rather like certain parts of Hesiod's *Works and Days.*

3. The following remarks assume the interpretation of the initial sentence proposed in Chapter Six, namely, that it applies to both intentional and unintentional homicide. The alternative assumption, that a brief statement of the penalty (exile) for intentional homi-

Πρῶτος Ἄξων

I.1. καὶ ἐὰν μὴ 'κ προνοίας κτείνῃ τίς τινα, φεύγειν.
2. δικάζειν δὲ τοὺς βασιλέας αἴτιον φόνου εἶναι τὸν ἐργασάμενον ἢ βουλεύσαντα. τοὺς δὲ ἐφέτας διαγνῶναι.
3. αἰδέσασθαι δ᾽ ἐὰν μὲν πατὴρ ᾖ ἢ ἀδελφὸς ἢ υἱεῖς ἅπαντας, ἢ τὸν κωλύοντα κρατεῖν. ἐὰν δὲ μὴ οὗτοι ὦσι, μέχρ᾽ ἀνεψιότητος καὶ ἀνεψιοῦ, ἐὰν ἅπαντες αἰδέσασθαι ἐθέλωσι, τὸν κωλύοντα κρατεῖν. ἐὰν δὲ τούτων μηδὲ εἷς ᾖ, κτείνῃ δὲ ἄκων, γνῶσι δὲ οἱ πεντήκοντα καὶ εἷς οἱ ἐφέται ἄκοντα κτεῖναι, ἐσέσθων δὲ οἱ φράτορες ἐὰν ἐθέλωσι δέκα. τούτους δὲ οἱ πεντήκοντα καὶ εἷς ἀριστίνδην αἱρείσθων. καὶ οἱ δὲ πρότερον κτείναντες ἐν τῷδε τῷ θεσμῷ ἐνεχέσθων.
II.4. προειπεῖν δὲ τῷ κτείναντι ἐν ἀγορᾷ μέχρ᾽ ἀνεψιότητος καὶ ἀνεψιοῦ.
5. συνδιώκειν δὲ κἀνεψιοὺς καὶ ἀνεψιῶν παῖδας καὶ γαμβροὺς καὶ πενθεροὺς καὶ φράτορας.
6. (protection before trial)
7. (safe passage into exile)
8. ἐὰν δέ τις τὸν ἀνδροφόνον κτείνῃ ἢ αἴτιος ᾖ φόνου ἀπεχόμενον ἀγορᾶς ἐφορίας καὶ ἄθλων καὶ ἱερῶν Ἀμφικτυονικῶν, ὥσπερ τὸν Ἀθηναῖον κτείναντα ἐν τοῖς αὐτοῖς ἐνέχεσθαι. διαγιγνώσκειν δὲ τοὺς ἐφέτας.
9. [ἐξ]εῖ[ναι δὲ τοὺς ἀνδροφόνους ἀποκτείνειν ἢ ἀπάγειν, ἐὰν ἐν] τῇ ἡμεδ[απῇ . . .]
III.10. (self-defense) . . . διαγιγνώσκειν δὲ τοὺς ἐφέτας.
11. [ἐὰν δέ τις . . .] ἢ ἐλεύθερος ᾖ, καὶ ἐὰν φέροντα ἢ ἄγοντα βίᾳ ἀδίκως εὐθὺς ἀμυνόμενος κτείνῃ, νηποινεὶ τεθνάναι.

The first section presents three essential aspects of the treatment of homicide: the penalty, the basic legal procedure, and the possibility of pardon. It is likely that before Drakon there existed two primary methods of dealing with homicide, exile and compensation (see above, Chapter Two). These two methods are not necessarily incompatible, since a killer might try to arrange for compensation either before or after going into exile; but uncertainty and confusion could easily arise, and sooner or later there would probably be a need for a clear and relatively simple procedure that could integrate the two systems and eliminate the confusion. Such a procedure is set forth in this first section, which posits exile as the primary penalty for a homicide but allows for pardon (usually achieved through compensation) if the victim's relatives agree.

The order of the provisions in this section implies that exile is to be the primary penalty for a homicide. The advantage of the priority of exile over compensation is evident: the killer is removed from contact with the victim's relatives as quickly as possible, thereby reducing the possibility of further hostility or bloodshed. Even if the relatives were allowed to agree to compensation before the trial or before the killer's exile, it would still be the killer's responsibility to go into exile if he could not reach a formal agreement with the relatives, who were under no obligation to accept or even to discuss compensation.

Drakon's second provision seems to treat two different matters. First it states the basic fact of trial by the kings and the Ephetai, and then it declares the planner of a homicide equally culpable. These are both important elements of the law, but the fact that the provision begins with the

---

cide originally preceded the preserved text, would not significantly alter the discussion.

verb δικάζειν and ends with the verb διαγνῶναι indicates
that providing for a trial is the primary concern. Since the
trial depicted on Achilles' shield concerns the payment
of compensation for a homicide, not the homicide itself
(εἵνεκα ποινῆς, Il. 18.498), we have no evidence for actual
homicide trials before Drakon. Nonetheless, it is possible
that such trials were held in early Athens either by voluntary agreement of both parties or under some sort of
civic sanction, and the absence of details in Drakon's law
concerning the trial, the kings, or the Ephetai may suggest that the process was a familiar one. Whatever the
procedural details, the provision for a trial is obviously an
important feature and belongs near the beginning of the
law. Like the penalty of exile, it too ought to reduce the
likelihood of conflict that might otherwise arise in a dispute about the identity of the killer.

The statement that the planner of a homicide is equally
culpable is also important, but its insertion here may seem
almost arbitrary. The rule could be mentioned in a number
of different places in the law, either earlier (by adding,
e.g., ἡ αἴτιος ἦ φόνου to the first protasis), or later as a separate provision (cf. And. 1.94). If it were located later in
the law, its absence from the first section would not seri-
ously affect the content of this section, whereas the provision for a trial must come early in the law. By introducing
the rule about the planner of a homicide in the first section
of his law, Drakon seems to be indicating its importance,
but by incorporating it in the provision for a trial rather
than writing it as a separate provision he maintains the
clear structure of this section, which systematically emphasizes the main points of the treatment of homicide: the
penalty, the trial, and pardon.

The third provision (or group of provisions) concerns
pardon and is retroactive.[4] I have already argued that the

---

4. Since the statement of retroactivity in lines 19–20 applies

details of this provision are probably new, and I suggested that they may have been inspired by the confusion which would have existed earlier if tradition held that compensation should be paid simply to "the relatives" (see above, pp. 15–16). The details in Drakon's law make it clear beyond question how such disputes are to be resolved, and again the advantage of requiring unanimity instead of allowing one relative or a majority of relatives to agree to pardon is evident. Allowing some of the relatives to make an agreement in the face of opposition by others would be likely to exacerbate the hostile feelings and would also raise the possibility that a relative who did not agree with the decision might seek his own private vengeance. We should keep in mind, moreover, that unanimity was probably more easily achieved in the more closely knit families of early Greece than it would be today.

It may seem incongruous that the provision for pardon is stated in such detail and at such length in contrast to the concise expression of the first two provisions, which seem equally or more important. The length or amount of detail of a provision, however, depends not on its importance but on certain other factors, such as the inherent complexity of the provision and perhaps the degree of innovation in it. Thus, the specification of details in the provision for pardon is necessary to preclude conflicts in the new system of compensation. On the other hand, the penalty of exile for homicide was probably a familiar one requiring no further elaboration. We can infer, then, that the procedure of trial by a court of the Ephetai presided over by the basileis was already familiar to Drakon's readers, since otherwise he would probably have

---

specifically to the rules for pardon (see above, chap. 3), I include it with them as one provision. Aly, p. 12, separates the three statements about pardon (his provisions 3, 4, and 5) but includes the statement of retroactivity as part of the last of these.

furnished more details concerning this procedure. It is not impossible that there is some significant innovation in this provision and that, for example, Drakon may have instituted the Ephetai and specified the composition of this body later in the law. But it seems more likely that if the Ephetai were a new body, Drakon would have designated their composition when he first mentions them, just as he designates the selection of the ten phratry members right after he mentions their function, rather than later in the law.

In sum, the first section of Drakon's law states the essential points of Drakon's treatment of homicide: the penalty, the trial, and the possibility of pardon. In a clear and intelligent manner it brings order to a system that probably contained potential for further conflict after a homicide. And the retroactivity of the provision for pardon extends this orderly solution to situations arising out of earlier homicides, some of which might not otherwise be resolved until several generations after Drakon.

The second section probably contained six provisions, of which three can be restored, setting forth the steps to be taken by the killer and the victim's relatives after a homicide. If the suggestions I have made for provisions 6, 7, and 9 are generally correct (see above, Chapter Three), then the six provisions are arranged in a logical order, beginning with the first steps to be taken by the relatives after the homicide: (4) the proclamation against the killer, (5) prosecution, (6) protection of the killer before the trial, (7) safe passage into exile, (8) protection of the killer in exile, and (9) the absence of protection for the killer who returns from exile.

These provisions all serve the basic goal of providing fair treatment both for the killer, who must be publicly notified of the accusation against him and is protected from harm as long as he observes the procedural rules set

forth, and for the relatives, who may obtain and enforce a
verdict of exile if they can persuade the court. The provisions also keep the killer and the relatives apart (except during the trial itself), thereby lessening the possibility of
further conflict.

As in the preceding section, details are provided where
necessary but are otherwise omitted. Thus, in the first
provision the proclamation is to be made "up to the degree
of first cousin once removed and first cousin." More
details are unnecessary, since it does not matter which relative or relatives make the proclamation, nor whether they
all agree. What is important is that at least one relative no-
tify the killer (and the public) that a formal accusation is
being made.

The next clause stipulates the various relatives who
with the phratry members are to "share in the prosecution"
($\sigma\upsilon\nu\delta\iota\dot{\omega}\kappa\epsilon\iota\nu$). The specific mention of cognate relatives
and phratry members was probably necessary because there
was no simpler way of indicating all these groups together.
It is notable that the relatives who would primarily be in
charge of the prosecution, presumably the victim's father,
brothers, and sons, are not mentioned. It is perhaps not
impossible that a statement of prosecution by these closer
relatives came later in the law, but there does not seem
to be any place for such a regulation in this section, and it
would be extremely odd to list these assistant prosecutors
here and postpone the mention of the primary prosecutors
until much later in the law. We must thus assume that the
requirement of prosecution by the closer relatives was self-
evident, probably because they traditionally were the
primary avengers of a homicide, and that the mention of
those who are to share in the prosecution implicitly confirms the assumption that prosecution is to be carried out
primarily by the unnamed closer relatives.

The only other fully restorable provision in this section

(lines 26–29) shows a similar pattern in that it includes several specific details but omits one important but self-evident fact. The clause provides protection for the convicted killer in exile as long as he keeps away from "frontier markets, games, and Amphiktyonic sacrifices." Drakon's intent here is probably to decrease the possibility of contact between the victim's relatives and the killer, and these three international meeting places are specifically mentioned in the law so that both parties will know the precise restrictions placed on the killer in exile.

The granting of protection to the killer only if he is in exile, however, is not specifically mentioned. True, the preceding provision may have specified how the killer should proceed into exile, but it is nonetheless remarkable that the qualification "in exile" or "outside Attica" is not stated in this provision. Again we must assume that the fact that the killer must be in exile in order to be protected by this law is so evident that it does not require specific mention.

After these two sections the law introduces certain exceptions to the basic treatment of homicide. The first of these, about which little can be said, apparently makes some allowances for killing in self-defense. The next concerns the lawful killing of an attacker. This provision specifies the circumstances under which the homicide is lawful: the attacker must be attempting by force and unjustly to seize the man's property or his person (for ransom), and the killing must be immediate and in self-defense. It is clear that the law places narrow limits on the circumstances of this lawful homicide, probably because Drakon is trying as much to deter the crime of unlawful seizure as to provide more lenient treatment for a certain kind of killing. Without the evidence of other provisions on lawful homicide that may have followed this

one, however, it is difficult to say much about Drakon's
purpose and method in this section.

So far we have noted one interesting stylistic feature
of Drakon's law, the coexistence of fullness of detail in
some places with brevity and even ellipsis in others.[5] Among
instances of the latter I would of course include the opening sentence of the law. The variation between brevity and
fullness seems to be determined by the requirements of
each provision, according to the general rule that details
are only included where necessary. In any case, whether
a provision is brief or full, the sense of the law is almost always clear, the provisions follow a coherent and sensible
order, and the treatment of both the killer and the victim's
family seems in every particular fair and intelligent.

Before proceeding with other stylistic considerations,
we should observe that if we accept the view that our
inscription accurately reproduces Drakon's actual words,
then we have here the earliest surviving example of Attic
prose and one of the earliest prose texts in any dialect.
This possibility is only rarely noted, probably because the
date 409/8 is so firmly attached to the inscription, because laws are not often thought of as prose texts, and because the text may seem unreliable.[6] But this text has at

---

5. Cf. Aly, pp. 18–19.

6. To my knowledge Aly is the only scholar who has discussed
Drakon's law as an example of early Attic prose style. His discussion
is vitiated, however, by the composite text he has assembled. Holger
Thesleff (*Arctos*, n.s. 4 [1966]: 100, n. 40) makes only a passing
reference to Drakon, and Bloch (p. 135, n. 3) considers the law "zu
verstümmelt überliefert" and refers to it only once (p. 139). Among
other scholars who examine Greek prose style, neither Eduard
Norden, *Die antike Kunstprosa* (Leipzig, 1915); Denniston, *GPS;*
C. Schick, *RFIC* 33 (1955): 361–90; nor S. Lilja, *On the Style
of the Earliest Greek Prose* (*Commentationes Humanarum Litterarum,*

least as good a claim to represent early Greek prose as do
the fragments of early historians and philosophers, none
of which has been preserved in such a direct transmission.
Yet the fragments of Pherekydes, Hekataios, Anaxagoras,
Heraklitos, and even Anaximander are scrutinized for clues
about early Greek prose style, whereas Drakon's law is
generally ignored. The stylistic features of this law thus
warrant consideration in greater detail.

The law is written as a number of successive provisions
that are relatively brief and essentially independent of
one another; that is, the substance of each provision is
self-contained, and almost any provision could be deleted
or put in a different place without substantially affect-
ing the content of the others (though of course the overall
effect of the law might be altered). They stand, as we
have seen, in a coherent order, each connected to the preceding provision by δέ. One stylistic feature in particular
helps make the organization by provisions clear, namely,
the use of an initial infinitive to introduce a provision. This
feature (which probably occurs in five of the eight restorable provisions)[7] simultaneously informs the reader that a
provision is beginning and in four cases specifies its topic.

---

vol. 41, no. 3 [1968]), mentions Drakon. Borimir Jordan maintains
that the Hekatompedon inscription (*IG* I^2.4 [I^3.4]) is a copy of a
sixth-century original and is thus "the oldest piece of connected, con-
tinuous Attic prose" (*Servants of the Gods* [*Hypomnemata,* vol. 55]
(Göttingen, 1979), p. 53). In making this claim he apparently over-
looks Drakon's law. He also neglects the possibility that the provisions
on the Hekatompedon inscription were originally enacted separately
and brought together only at the time of their re-publication, as is
indicated by the triple rows of dots between provisions and the
asyndeton at the beginning of each.

7. Stroud's suggested restoration of the ninth provision begins
with an infinitive, ἐξεῖναι. This may not be the correct beginning,
but the letter traces in the fourth stoichos of line 30 preclude the

This organization is different from the style of other surviving Greek laws, in which the provisions tend to be linked into rather long sections and the use of initial infinitives is relatively rare.[8] Provisions are most commonly introduced by a conditional clause either specifying a violation of the preceding provision or an alternative situation; in Drakon's law introductory conditional clauses are found only within the provisions for pardon and in the first and eighth provisions.[9] Any part of the Gortyn laws demonstrates this difference: there the most common connection is provided by αἰ δέ, and a new provision or section is generally indicated by asyndeton or an empty letter space or both.

Within the provisions of Drakon's law themselves we find one striking stylistic feature, the chiastic arrangement of subject (S) and verb (V) in conjoined clauses (i.e., SVVS or VSSV). This chiasmus occurs five times: δικάζειν δὲ τοὺς βασιλέας . . . τοὺς δὲ ἐφέτας διαγνῶναι (lines 11–13); αἰδέσασθαι . . . ἅπαντας ἢ τὸν κωλύοντα κρατεῖν (13–14); μηδὲ εἷς ᾖ, κτείνῃ δὲ ἄκων (16–17); ἐσέσθων δὲ οἱ φράτορες . . . οἱ πεντήκοντα καὶ εἷς . . . αἱρείσθων (18–19); ἐὰν δέ τις . . . ἐνέχεσθαι. διαγιγνώσκειν δὲ τοὺς ἐφέτας (26–29).[10] Particularly notable is the fact that Drakon varies a phrase that might be thought to be almost formulaic (τοὺς δὲ

---

possibility that the provision began with ἐὰν δέ (see Stroud, p. 12), and an infinitive beginning is thus most likely.

8. For initial infinitives in legal statements see, e.g., *GHI* 40.12, 16; 73.8, 34, 36; Gortyn VIII.7–8.

9. The eleventh provision may also have begun in line 36 with ἐὰν δέ; see above, chap. 3.

10. In lines 26–29 I take the subject of the verb ἐνέχεσθαι to be expressed by the conditional clause at the beginning. In lines 16–17 the adjective ἄκων serves stylistically to fill the place of the unexpressed subject.

ἐφέτας διαγνῶναι in line 13; διαγιγνώσκειν δὲ τοὺς ἐφέτας
in line 29) in order to achieve this chiastic effect.

In contrast to these instances of chiasmus, there are
only two instances of a parallel arrangement of subject and
verb in conjoined clauses (i.e., SVSV or VSVS),[11] and
both occur immediately after a chiasmus, resulting in a
longer connected sequence, either SVVSVS (μηδὲ εἷς
ᾖ, κτείνῃ δὲ ἄκων, γνῶσι δὲ οἱ πεντήκοντα καὶ εἷς, lines
16–17) or VSSVSV (ἐσέσθων δὲ οἱ φράτορες . . . οἱ
πεντήκοντα καὶ εἷς . . . αἱρείσθων. . . . οἱ δὲ πρότερον
κτείναντες . . . ἐνεχέσθων, lines 18–20).

The purpose of the chiastic arrangement seems to be
not to embellish the law with artistic effects but rather
to provide a clear structure to the various provisions. In
two cases (lines 11–13, 26–29) the chiasmus helps define
the end of a provision, and in one case (13–14) it defines
the end of one part of a provision. In the other two cases,
in which chiasmus is followed by a parallel arrangement,
the effect is to link the three verbs closely. This is especially
helpful in the conditional clause (lines 16–17), all three
parts of which must be fulfilled in order for pardon to be
granted by ten phratry members. Similarly, this arrangement more closely links the statement of reciprocity to the
end of the provisions for pardon (lines 18–20). Moreover,
in this latter case the connection is reinforced by the fact
that the three verbs are all third person imperatives and
are in fact the only imperatives in the law, which otherwise
uses the infinitive.

It is a common view that chiasmus is a characteristic
of early Greek prose,[12] and although the evidence is scarce

---

11. I describe this arrangement as parallel rather than symmetrical because the order SVVS seems to me more symmetrical than
SVSV; cf. Denniston, *GPS*, pp. 71–77.

12. See, e.g., Denniston, *GPS*, pp. 3, 127 ("the marked chiastic

and scholars have a regrettable tendency to include many examples from Heraklitos[13]–whose style can scarcely be considered typical–this judgment seems accurate.[14] More important, with the exception of Heraklitos early prose authors do not seem to use chiasmus in the same way as later authors, who use it mainly for sharpening a contrast or for variation when a word is repeated from one phrase to the next.[15] In early prose, on the other hand, we find chiasmus in most cases employed simply and almost casually.[16] I would not call the use of chiasmus in Drakon's law casual, but in comparison with later authors it is

---

bias of early prose"). Of course very little surviving Greek prose antedates the fifth century and none is as old as Drakon.

13. Denniston, *GPS*, pp. 3, 74, 127 cites Heraklitos fr. 88: τάδε γὰρ μεταπεσόντα ἐκεῖνά ἐστι, κἀκεῖνα πάλιν μεταπεσόντα ταῦτα. The syntactic arrangement of this sentence, however, is SPVSP[V] (where P = predicate), which is not at all chiastic. In fact Heraklitos prefers parallel syntax, which sometimes results in a semantic chiasmus, as above or in fr. 62: ἀθάνατοι θνητοί, θνητοὶ ἀθάνατοι (= SPSP). For syntactic chiasmus in Heraklitos see, e.g., the continuation of fr. 62: ζῶντες τὸν ἐκείνων θάνατον, τὸν δὲ ἐκείνων βίον τεθνεῶτες (= VOOV, where O = object).

14. Lilja (above, n. 6) includes examples of chiasmus (which she understands in a rather broad sense) from Heraklitos but also from other early authors, thereby lending greater weight to her conclusion that chiasmus is a common feature of these authors (p. 133).

15. See Denniston (*GPS*, pp. 74–77), who also finds examples of chiastic antitheses in the Ionian philosophers.

16. The closest parallel I have found to the kind of chiasmus in Drakon's law is Pherekydes of Athens, *FGH* 3 F135a: αἱ δὲ Ἐρινύες ἔρχονται ἐπ᾽ αὐτὸν [Orestes] θέλουσαι ἀποκτεῖναι, καὶ ἐρύκει αὐτὰς ἡ Ἄρτεμις. For the distinction between simple and artistic chiasmus see Bloch, p. 147. Schick (above, n. 6, p. 371) discusses one example of "la disposizione chiasmatica" in a law from Argos (*GD* 85, lines 35–36), but this is not an exact chiasmus, since the order is IoSVVO (where Io = Indirect object).

relatively simple,[17] and this feature can thus be considered an indication of the "archaic" nature of Drakon's prose style.[18]

The law also has a few other notable stylistic features. For example, Drakon sandwiches a conditional clause between verb and subject (αἰδέσασθαι δ᾽ ἐὰν μὲν πατὴρ ᾖ ἢ ἀδελφὸς ἢ υἱεῖς ἅπαντας, lines 13–14) or between a noun and its modifier (οἱ φράτορες ἐὰν ἐθέλωσι δέκα, line 18), giving emphasis in both cases to the postponed number. Moreover, two sentences in the provisions on pardon consist of two separate protases with one apodosis (lines 14–16, 16–18).[19] Another device is the threefold occurrence of the demonstrative pronoun οὗτοι . . . τούτων . . . τούτους to link closely several parts of the provisions for pardon.

One should also note that Drakon does not hesitate to combine items in a series,[20] a feature that if overused could quickly make the law monotonous but here seems to be kept under control. Smaller points of note are the absence of alliteration, the frequent occurrence of hiatus, and the apparently random use of elision and crasis.[21] The subjunctive is used throughout in the protases of conditions.[22] The aspectual difference between the aorist

---

17. Cf., e.g., Isok. 4.95: καλῶς ἀποθανεῖν ἢ ζῆν αἰσχρῶς.

18. These considerations may lend support to Ruschenbusch's view (see above, chap. 7, n. 52) that there is a chiastic arrangement of terms in Solon's amnesty decree.

19. Schick (above, n. 6, pp. 375–76) notes examples of this sentence structure at Gortyn.

20. πατὴρ . . . ἢ ἀδελφὸς ἢ υἱεῖς (lines 13–14), κἀνεψιοὺς καὶ ἀνεψιῶν παῖδας καὶ γαμβροὺς καὶ πενθεροὺς καὶ φράτορας (22–23), ἀγορᾶς ἐφορίας καὶ ἄθλων καὶ ἱερῶν Ἀμφικτυονικῶν (27–28).

21. Cf. δ᾽ ἐάν (line 13) and δὲ ἄκων (line 17); κἀνεψιοὺς καὶ ἀνεψιῶν (line 22).

22. Cf. the Gortyn laws, in which the ratio of subjunctives to optatives is eighty to fifty (Willetts, p. 7).

and present infinitives is generally observed, but for no apparent reason seems to be violated in the second provision of the law (δικάζειν) and perhaps also in the eighth and tenth (διαγιγνώσκειν).[23]

From these considerations it is evident that Drakon consciously incorporated stylistic features not simply for artistic effect, but as part of an effort to write a clear, coherent, well-organized, and effective homicide law. The stylistic features help to clarify not only the order of the whole law but also the internal structure and intent of the provisions.

The elegance of Drakon's law is especially apparent in contrast to the few other surviving laws of the seventh or sixth centuries, which seem to be organized primarily in the form of a statement of a regulation followed by the sanctions for violating that regulation. The earliest Cretan law from Dreros (*GD* 116 = *GHI* 2), for example, has precisely this structure,[24] and an early treaty from Elis (*GD* 62 = *GHI* 17) reveals an extension of the same structure: first a statement of the treaty, then an elaboration of the requirements of the treaty, and finally two sentences in case of violations of the treaty. The last three sentences all begin αἰ δέ.[25]

Another early law from Elis, the Elean *rhetra* (*GD* 61), repeats this structure twice:[26] first a statement of

23. See above, chap. 3, n. 47.

24. The last line of *GD* 116 is separated from the rest of the law by a special mark indicating a new section. It is not clear whether the statement in this last line has any connection with the other provisions on the inscription.

25. Cf. *GD* 64, another early Elean law (apparently the continuation of a set of regulations separately inscribed), in which a regulation is followed by another provision concerning a violation of the regulation and then by two further regulations.

26. I follow Buck's interpretation of the opening lines of this much disputed *rhetra*. For a full discussion with references to other

protection for an accused person is followed by two conditional sanctions in case this protection is violated (lines 1–5), and then a statement that certain officials shall enforce this law is followed by three more sanctions (lines 5–9). These last three sanctions, however, have a more complex structure: the second of them has two protases, one before and one after the apodosis (cf. above, n. 19), and in the third sentence the apodosis (A) comes before the protasis (P). This arrangement produces the structure PA–PAP–AP, which is almost as elaborate as in the provisions for pardon in Drakon's law and may indicate a similar attempt to give variation to the expression of a series of conditional sentences.

The Elean *rhetra* presents another similarity to Drakon's law, namely, a considerable ellipsis in the opening sentence: πατριὰν θαρρέν καὶ γενεὰν καὶ ταὐτō–"His gens is to be protected and his family and his property."[27] It is not immediately apparent what this regulation refers to, but the prevailing view is that it applies to the gens, family, and property of an accused man. The omission of any reference to an accused person, however, is a striking example of the tendency to conciseness of expression which is characteristic of early law and which we have already noted in Drakon's law.[28]

In comparison with these other early laws, the organi-

---

views see Glotz (pp. 247–59), who differs from Buck in his interpretation of the second sentence. See also L. H. Jeffery, *The Local Scripts of Archaic Greece* (Oxford, 1961), p. 218 and n. 5, who dates the *rhetra* to the early fifth century and interprets the whole text differently from Glotz, Buck, et al.

27. For the sense see Glotz, pp. 254–58.

28. There may be a similar ellipsis in *GD* 65 (fourth century). This begins ταὶρ δὲ γενεαὶρ μὰ φυγαδείημ, which Buck translates "But one shall not exile the children (of an exile)." Buck argues that the qualification "of an exile" would have been understood

zation of Drakon's law is more varied and his style more
elegant; moreover, his ellipses are never as obscure as that
in the opening of the Elean *rhetra*. This should not be
taken as an indication that the preserved text of the homicide law is the product of revision at a later date, because
Drakon's law also differs from later Greek laws. We need
read only a little way into the Gortyn laws, for example, to
realize how different their monotonous, parallel syntac-
tical arrangement is from Drakon's These laws are apparently a compendium of previously existing legislation
with little overall organization and almost no stylistic
elegance.

The outstanding characteristics of Drakon's law suggest
several conclusions: first, that the author of the homicide
law made a conscious effort to write a clear, well-organized,
and stylistically pleasing law; second, that the law in its
present form is almost certainly the product of a single
author and not the result of piecemeal revision or the com-
pilation of traditional provisions; third, that this author
was an unusually gifted individual; and fourth, that the
author is much more likely to have been Drakon than some
anonymous sixth- or fifth-century official.

Our final observations concern the general nature of
Drakon's homicide law in the context of the history of
Athenian law and legal procedure. We have already noted
in a number of cases that a certain provision was or was
not likely to be traditional, and I suggested that where Drakon is relatively brief he is more likely to be conforming
to the traditional practice, but that where he includes a
number of specific details he is probably making some innovation. Of course we cannot be certain in many cases
whether a provision is new or traditional, but the evidence

---

from a law that preceded this one, but it seems possible that it is
meant to be supplied from the content of this law alone.

suggests that Drakon incorporated a great many features
of the traditional treatment of homicide in his law. Even
where he apparently made innovations, such as in the provisions for pardon, he did not radically alter the traditional practice but rather refined it so as to make the
regulations clearer and more effective.

Whatever the extent of innovation, the essential nature
of Drakon's homicide legislation is apparent in the surviving provisions. These provisions suggest a number of
interesting conclusions, of which perhaps the most important concerns the dispute about the evolution of Greek
legal procedure from a form of voluntary arbitration to
a compulsory legal procedure.

The traditional view, articulated most fully by Steinwenter,[29] is that the transition was relatively simple and
direct; voluntary arbitration became more and more common and was eventually made compulsory, first by the
power of the nobles and then by law. The transition was
more or less complete by the time of Homer (as seen
in the trial scene on Achilles' shield) and Hesiod, when
arbitration was still practiced (as it was also in the
fourth century) but self-help had virtually disappeared.
Against this view Wolff has argued for an intermediate
stage of development (revealed in Homer, Hesiod, and Drakon's law) in which the judicial authorities were "charged
with supervising the use of private force by individuals,"
or, in other words, "merely allowed or forbade self-help"
(pp. 76–77).[30]

In my view the evidence of Drakon's law lends some
support to both sides. The basic treatment of homicide in
Drakon's law is a trial with the penalty of exile for con-

---

29. See also Hildebrecht Hommel, *Palingenesia* 4 (1969):11–38.
30. See also Louis Gernet, *Droit et société dans la Grèce ancienne*
(Paris, 1955), pp. 61–81, and Harrison, vol. 2, pp. 69–72.

viction. This in itself indicates that the magistrates have a certain judicial authority and that a verdict is a statement of a judicial punishment and not simply an acknowledgment of the prosecutor's right to use self-help.[31] Furthermore, the fact that the state guarantees the exiled killer's safety (provided he observes certain restrictions) shows conclusively that a verdict of guilty does not certify the prosecutors' right to use self-help but in fact denies that right as long as the convicted killer observes the terms of his punishment.

On the other hand, self-help continues to be an important part of the system. The victim's relatives must themselves make the proclamation and carry out the prosecution. Furthermore, they are charged with overseeing the penalty in the sense that if the convicted killer does not obey the regulations governing his exile, they are allowed to do as they wish with him. They are also allowed to pardon him if they wish. In all these respects the system of self-help provides considerable support for the compulsory judicial procedure. We might also note that the provision for lawful homicide in lines 36–38 in effect authorizes the use of self-help under certain specific circumstances, but this use is authorized by the law and not by a court's verdict.

Thus, Drakon's law reveals a system of compulsory trial and sentencing in cases of homicide, supported by self-help on the part of the victim's relatives. In other words, the Athenian legal system has by this time incorporated the system of self-help into a system of compulsory legal procedure. The system makes extensive use of self-help, but the subordination of self-help to the judicial process is clear.

---

31. If one accepts Wolff's view, one can assume that the alleged lost provision on intentional homicide did not state any penalty for this offense but simply allowed self-help to run its course in such cases. See Ruschenbusch, "*phonos*," p. 145, n. 74.

This system persists in several ways into the fourth century,[32] when both the prosecution of a case and the enforcement of a verdict must still in many cases be undertaken by the victim himself (or his relatives). The legal system becomes more comprehensive than in the seventh century, but self-help continues to be an essential part of the compulsory, state-controlled judicial process.

Certain other general features of Drakon's homicide law are also notable. First, the law indicates that the "solidarity of the family" is beginning to weaken, as may already be indicated by the trial scene on Achilles' shield. Glotz (p. 324) remarks that the division of the relatives into two groups for the purpose of granting pardon is a sign of decreasing unity, and we should add that the requirement for unanimity in each group implies that even in these smaller groups of relatives unanimity could not be taken for granted. The family still plays an important role in homicide cases, but it is beginning to be seen as a collection of individual members rather than as a single unit.

On the other hand, the unity of the polis is taken for granted. The penalty of exile, without further specification, implies that the polis was a recognized geographical entity, and this implication is supported by the phrase [ἐν] τῆ ἡμεδ[απῆ] (lines 30–31). Moreover, the provision protecting the exiled killer (lines 26–29) implies that disputes might previously have arisen concerning the killer's presence at the frontier markets but not at other points along the border, for otherwise some description of the border would have been included in the law.

Finally, we should note that the preserved provisions are entirely secular and contain no indication of any religious origin or purpose. It may be impossible to disprove

---

32. Cf. Hansen, pp. 113–21.

beyond doubt a claim that, for example, the penalty of exile was inspired by a religious concern with the pollution of the city, [33] but if such was the case, Drakon has carefully avoided any suggestion of this concern in the wording of his law. In my view he was motivated by no such concern. [34]

In the most thorough study of the question of religious pollution, Moulinier (esp. pp. 43–46) searches at length for some indication that Drakon spoke of the killer's pollution, and after rejecting several passages from the orators he settles on two passages from the fourth century as evidence for a tradition of religious pollution going back to Drakon. The first, Plato *Laws* 865E, which states that the unintentional killer must abstain from his victim's customary haunts for a year, is (according to Moulinier) based on tradition. But even if Plato's views are based on tradition,

---

33. Although the exiling of a killer does not necessarily imply that he was thought to be polluted, the casting of an object adjudged responsible for homicide beyond the borders of Attica suggests that the object was thought harmful to the polis on account of its pollution. This practice is attested only by Pollux (8.120) and the Patmos scholion *ad* Dem. 23.76 (see *BCH* 1 [1877]:139); neither source indicates how old the practice is and we have no reason to think it goes back to Drakon. Even if it does, the trial of an object may have arisen simply as a symbolic substitute for the trial and subsequent exile of the unknown thrower of the object.

34. MacDowell, pp. 141–50, has an excellent discussion of the difficulty of knowing the motive behind any of the homicide laws. He rejects as unprovable any attempts to make religious pollution the underlying motive of Athenian homicide law, noting that only the provision requiring purification when a pardoned killer returns from exile (Dem. 23.72) proves that the doctrine of pollution was recognized anywhere in the law. We have no reason to think that this provision goes back to Drakon.

this tradition need not go back to Drakon, nor need it be based on a concept of religious pollution. We should note, moreover, that whereas Plato's regular formula for lawful homicide is to declare the killer pure (καθαρὸς ἔστω, 865B2, etc.), actual Athenian laws use secular expressions such as Drakon's νηποινεὶ τεθνάναι.[35]

Moulinier's second piece of evidence for this tradition is a passage in which Demosthenes (23.40) claims that in the provision protecting the exiled killer who abstains from frontier markets, games, and Amphiktyonic sacrifices, Drakon "keeps the killer away from everything in which the victim participated in his lifetime" (ὅσων τῷ παθόντι ζῶντι μετῆν, τούτων εἴργει τὸν δεδρακότα). But even if Demosthenes is accurately representing Drakon's motive (and there is no reason to believe he is), Drakon's basic purpose may just as well be to appease the victim's relatives (or his spirit in Hades) as to satisfy some demand of religious pollution.

Finally, Moulinier's general argument is that only public opinion, stimulated by the fear of the killer's pollution, could have given the polis enough support to encroach on the traditional power of the clans. Though impossible to disprove, this claim is not supported by any evidence and seems quite implausible. The need for a judicial system under the control of the state would be felt as soon as the system of self-help was perceived to be inadequate to deal with all contingencies. Sentiments favoring public law and order are understandable in themselves and do not require a religious explanation.

---

35. See the laws cited in And. 1.96; *Ath. Pol.* 16.10; Dem. 23.28, 23.53 (cf. 24.113). The orators occasionally use the word καθαρός (e.g., Dem. 20.158, Lyk. 125), and Eukrates' decree (passed in 336) declares that anyone killing a tyrant shall be "pure" (ὅσιος ἔστω, *SEG* 12.87.11).

Moreover, every provision of Drakon's law is easily
explained on secular grounds. Exile of the killer and restrictions against his visiting the frontier markets, etc., are
the surest way to prevent further conflict between him
and the victim's family. Pardon, if agreed to unanimously,
would allow the killer's return without any further danger
of conflict. And the initial proclamation against the killer
would be necessary to inform him of the charge so that he
could defend himself. The secular need for all these provisions is clear.

Moreover, the argument *ex silentio* has some force,
since we would expect some mention, say, of the necessity
for purification after pardon, if such a requirement existed.
But neither here nor in the provision for exile (where the
killer's pollution might be mentioned) nor in the provision
for a proclamation (where banishment from certain religious places or events might be mentioned)[36] is there any
hint of an underlying idea of religious pollution. This
comprehensive silence does much to discredit the hypothesis that the concept of pollution for homicide had any
influence on Drakon's law.

In sum, the preserved provisions of Drakon's law reveal
an effective approach to the problems of homicide law, a
clear and orderly structure, and an elegance of expression
that make it a model of its kind. Indeed, the law was so
effective that Solon left it unchanged, and several centuries

---

36. We do not know whether Drakon specified an exact form
for the proclamation against a killer; most later references use the
expression εἴργειν τῶν νομίμων (e.g., Ant. 6.35). Demosthenes' list
(20.158) of places from which the killer was excluded (which may
reflect Drakon's language) includes religious as well as secular places,
but these are probably included because they are public places
where the victim's relatives might otherwise come into contact with
the killer.

later it still formed the essence of Athenian homicide law. Later tradition has continued to remember Drakon primarily for the severity of his punishments. But his surviving fragment suggests a different judgment, for at least with respect to homicide the first Athenian lawgiver bestowed upon his city a fair and effective law, notable for its style as well as its content.

INDEX LOCORUM

GENERAL INDEX